Advance Pra: !ing
relationships li!

"*Four paws up for **the Boston rules, building relationships
like a dog!** A 1% change in 100 things will make a significant
improvement in your valued relationships. This principle is
easily adapted to both personal and professional relationships.
I would love to see it implemented in our sales training!*
—*Karen Carini*
*Regional Senior Sales Manager, Fairmont Hotels & Resorts,
Canada's Western Mountain Region*

"*This captivating, little book is packed with examples for how
we can better relate to each other based on insightful teachings
from dogs. Love it!*"
—*Dr. Judith Samson-French, BSc MSc DVM*

"*Find a comfy seat, and set aside a couple of hours—I challenge
you not to read **the Boston rules** cover to cover in one sitting! I
was captivated by how the Boston rules simplify and eloquently
capture how to build better relationships, ultimately driving
client and employee loyalty.*"
— *Jeff Fisher, Retired BMO*

the
BOSTON
rules

building relationships like a dog

the BOSTON

rules

building relationships like a dog

Richard and Lana Casavant

the Boston rules Media

DEDICATION

To Dickens,
our beloved Boston

Beyond loving. Beyond faithful. Beyond dedicated.
Taken from us by cancer at the young age of ten, you and our
other pets taught us much about life.
Living your lessons, you're forever in our hearts . . .

Mom & Dad

Thoughts before you dig in!

"'Everything happens for a reason' is the mantra by which Lana and I live our lives—good or bad, everything happens for a reason."

—Richard Casavant

In 2003, Lana left a city full of friends she loved and adored, moving from Calgary, Alberta, to beautiful Vancouver, British Columbia, Canada, with Dickens and Skeeter to start a new adventure—an adventure that would change both of our lives.

One of her first business trips was to attend a SKI TOPS conference in Alyeska, Alaska, and, boy, did that turn out to be fortunate! We bumped into each other, and our introduction was life changing, resulting with my packing up Katie and Kaizer, my two German shepherds, for a move from St. Petersburg, Florida, to Vancouver. Six months later?

Married!

Since that time, the list of 'everything happens for a reason' gets longer and longer. Here are just a few:

- Lana left Calgary, and attended the event, SKI TOPS—otherwise, we wouldn't have met.

- During my introduction at the conference, I shared I train dogs—otherwise, we wouldn't have been presented with a common denominator from which our connection and love grew.

- Dickens wouldn't poop in the rain, and Lana needed help training him!

- Lana's sister, Lynne, had room on her acreage in Oregon to care for Katie and Kaizer while we found a home to rent in Vancouver. That wasn't easy! With four pets? Not likely! But, luckily, we found just the right place—otherwise, it wouldn't have been possible for me to pack up my dogs, and head north.

- Our wonderful landlord, who owned the perfect dog home half a block from a forest, was willing to give our family of two large dogs, one small dog, and our kitty a chance in a city that loves animals, but doesn't want to rent to them.

• Dickens, our Boston, died of cancer before his tenth birthday, leaving a huge void in our lives, resulting in our desire to share in a book the many gifts he taught us.

• Skeeter, our kitty, died at the glorious age of twenty-one, just two weeks before Cheddar turned up at the trucking company of my brother-in-law, George—Cheddar needed a family. We wouldn't have accepted him had Skeeter still been with us.

And, the list goes on.

The beauty about this book is you don't have to read from beginning to end for it to make sense. Find a rule that pertains to your life and situation—dog ear the pages! Highlight! Underline! Use it as the little book that can make a huge difference in your day—any day of the week!

We hope the lessons our many animals taught us—those we share in *the Boston rules—building relationships like a dog*—inspire you to look to your own pets for inspiration. Try adopting some of our lessons learned to build better relationships to make our world a little kinder, one person at a time.

We hope you enjoy the book!

Rule #1

Welcome! Welcome! Welcome!

"Each one of our dogs makes us feel as if we're the center of their universe—every day, all day."

—Anonymous

Just think—if all of us mimic a dog's intensity, love, loyalty, and devotion, doesn't it make you wonder how different our relationships would be? When you walk through the door, who's the first person—or, pet—to greet you? In our family, it's our dogs. But, what if we greeted our spouses, children, and family at the door like our dogs do? How do you think they'd feel?

One of my favorite memories of Dickens is when Lana would return home from work late in the afternoon. Whenever he heard the front door open, he'd jump up and race to the door, his little Flintstone legs skittering on the hardwood floors, rounding corners like a greyhound, then finally skidding to a stop in front of the door, or leaping into his mom's arms—unless I got there first!

If both of us heard the door, the game was on and, on more than one occasion, Lana would come in the front door, looking down to find a tumble of legs, arms (mine), and wriggling bodies trying to be the first to get to her. Yesterday, it was Dickens. Today, it's Barclay, racing me to the door to give the first kiss as we listen for the sound of her key—or, as she listens for mine—so we can greet each other at the door. I miss that game with Dickens, but I love the game with Barclay. I'm grateful both continue to teach me the importance of *Welcome! Welcome! Welcome!* and how important it is to be desired, wanted, and appreciated.

When we share the story about how we race to the front door, most people can't relate to it for two reasons—first, they don't do it for their family and, second, their family doesn't do it for them. When many of us walk in the front door, our spouses or kids don't stop what they're doing to meet us, although, over the years, we have met a few couples who say, "I do that . . ." Good for them for *building relationships like a dog*! For others, however, it hasn't occurred to them to follow our pets' examples—Dickens taught his behavior to Skeeter, and Barclay taught it to Cheddar.

Of course, cats may not be known as great doormen, but, since our cats raised our Bostons, it was natural for them to build their relationships like a dog, adopting routines paying off with lots of loving at the door. When Skeeter, our delicate nine pounds of calico love, heard us coming in the house, she would make her way to the front door to say hello to receive her loving reward. Not wanting to miss out on the hello celebration, she would sit quietly in the background waiting for the chaos to subside as her bigger brothers and sister expressed their happiness at our arrival. When wagging tails and bouncing bodies calmed down, she gently approached us with her standard high-five greeting, ready to accept a gentle caress. Long after she experienced the sadness of losing her pack, Skeeter continued to faithfully meet us at the door until the end of her twenty-one years.

We remember with tremendous fondness how much we looked forward to being welcomed home and, for anyone who's had a best friend meet them at the door, then lost them, you know the gift they gave as well as the void they left. For us, *Welcome! Welcome! Welcome!* is a rule we never want to take for granted.

We shared this 'best practice' many times with audiences around the world and, on one occasion, Lana shared the story of the race to the door with a woman she met at a conference.

After hearing our experience and with tears in her eyes, the woman said, "I never stop what I'm doing to greet my mom at the door when she visits." She paused. "I never stop what I'm doing to greet my husband—but, when my nieces or nephews come over, I race to the door to greet them and shower them with hugs and kisses." Reflecting quietly, she asked, "What's the message I'm sending to my mom, and to my husband? That I take them for granted?" A few more tears, and a moment to reflect. "I can't wait," she continued, "until my husband comes home—or, the next time my mom comes over—to greet them at the door, showing them my appreciation. I think they'll be so surprised—my mom may shed a tear . . ."

Are you doing the same thing? The woman's practice of greeting her nieces and nephews—but, not her mom or husband—was her habit, and probably behavior many of us exhibit. Dickens's and every other dog's demonstration of love provides us with an example of a one percent adjustment in our behavior that will have a one hundred percent impact on relationships around us.

How much do you look forward to your dog greeting you? And, how much would you like someone in your family to acknowledge your arrival? Trust us—it trickles into all kinds of other thoughtful aspects of consideration.

While living in Vancouver, we realized the significance of our pets' welcoming us, and we changed our behavior toward our two German shepherds, Katie and Kaizer, who consistently met us at the side gate. We would say hello to them as we went up the stairs, instead of taking the extra fifteen steps to properly greet them. Realizing what we were doing (or, not doing), as we turned and headed toward the front door, we could hear K2 rounding the back corner of the house where we'd let them into the kitchen for a proper welcome. Good heavens! How could we have missed their intention?

Lana and I instantly changed our behavior by one percent by going to them and saying a sincere hello, sticking our hands through the gate to scratch a head, or get a finger lick.

What a lesson they taught us!

When Dickens was a puppy, Lana established 'Canine Fridays' at her office. She would zoom home at noon to pick him up to bring him back for the afternoon. Being a Boston terrier herself, it didn't occur to her to ask for permission, nor did it matter to her Dickens was the only canine who tended to show up on the unofficial celebration day.

No one was surprised when Lana blasted out of the office on Friday afternoon, the receptionist always looking forward to welcoming Dickens when they returned. Lana and Dickens stopped at reception to say hello, giving her a chance to call Lana's colleague and best friend, informing her of the impending greeting. Danette would step out of her office, positioning herself at the end of the hall with wide-open arms, anticipating the storm hurtling toward her. As Dickens rounded the corner, he would take one look at the woman who was his second mom, race down the hall, and shower her with kisses.

After Dickens was welcomed, welcomed, welcomed, he and Lana took time to circle the entire office, saying hello to all of his people friends. Lana's colleagues told her when they heard the jingle of his collar, they knew Dickens was on his way to make their day.

Sometimes, at the office, just like Dickens, the president of the company would take the time to walk around and say hello to everyone, asking how they were. It left them feeling valued, and appreciated. The point is how special do we feel when someone takes the time to say hello?

Remember—*Welcome! Welcome! Welcome!* works both ways. It's just that our pets do it naturally . . .

So can we.

When people walk into your business or office space, try glancing their way to acknowledge their presence. Share a quick smile, a warm hello, or stand up to greet them—it says we respect and appreciate them. At work, when you poke your head into a person's office each day to say hello, it shows them their value as part of the team. When you walk by someone and smile, say their name, or ask them what's new—it affirms their self-worth. The cool thing is it doesn't take much time, and a little attention can make a huge impact on other people's lives.

In our minds, important *Rule #1, Welcome! Welcome! Welcome!* points to our everyday behaviors and common-sense opportunities we typically don't consider. As I say in my training courses and keynote addresses, we shouldn't be looking for a one hundred percent improvement in one thing. In fact, it's just the opposite—we should be looking for a one percent improvement in one hundred things.

So, here's the basic question to consider if you're interested in making a one percent change in your behavior that will have a hundred percent impact on another person:

Are you giving your best to your spouse and family, or do

you save it for friends and strangers?

We try to be as constant as our pets by consistently providing a 'paw'sitive' welcome to those around us. After all, have your dogs ever greeted you at the door in a bad mood? I respectfully submit they have not, and never will . . .

Here's the upshot of *Rule #1, Welcome! Welcome! Welcome!* Our pets give us their best expressions, their best tone of voice, and their best welcome—all the time.

Do we?

Home is where someone runs to meet you . . .

Rule #2

Accept Others as They Are

*"Our job on earth isn't to criticize, reject, or judge. Our
purpose is to offer a helping hand, compassion, and mercy.
We are to do unto others as we hope they would do unto us."*

—Dana Arcuri, Harvest of Hope:
Living Victoriously Through Adversity

What do you think of when you consider these two
words—acceptance and tolerance? Of course, you
know both terms relate to attitudes which convey
patience and respect for practices or people. 'Acceptance'
is when you experience a situation, and you don't resist it.
'Tolerance' is when you allow the existence, occurrence, or
practice of something—or, someone—without interference,

even though you don't necessarily agree.

Think about it—you're aware of acceptance and tolerance every day, although you don't actively think about either one. Our dogs, however, don't distinguish the difference between the two, and they show it through interesting and, sometimes, unlikely friendships. When dogs meet, one seems to size up the other—tails or no tails, big or small, short or long hair, they don't seem to care. They appear to base their likes and dislikes on attitude—or, how other dogs accept them.

If a dog is overly aggressive or lacks respect, there may be a reaction. But, if their new acquaintance is friendly and nice? They establish friendships, regardless of social status or appearance, and they're open to learning. Conversely, when we don't accept someone who is different from us, we lose the ability and opportunity to learn about the other person, as well as ourselves.

If you're a movie buff, you may recall the 1960 black and white film, *Inherit the Wind*—it fictionalized the 'Scopes Monkey Trial' which took place in Tennessee in 1925. Attorney Dudley Field Malone defended the right to teach science in schools, and I'll never forget part of his speech in the movie (paraphrasing, of course—my memory isn't that good!)

We have never learned anything from anyone who agrees with us!

I believe it! Meeting new people, as well as learning different practices, teaches us acceptability and tolerance. Apparently, dogs already know that! The question is how can *we* learn to *accept others as they are?*

Quick story—when my first wife and I were raising our kids in Littleton, Colorado, one of my favorite places to work was Peaberry's Coffee. When I walked into the coffee shop and stood in line to order, I always looked at the four profiles of coffee based on personality—or, is it four profiles of personalities based on coffee?

Interestingly, the four Peaberry Profiles cover the four major personality types according to most personality-based assessments. Personality tests—ranging from the silly to the dead serious—are booming online, and do you know why? Because everyone is interested in themselves! That's according to the CEO of a leading Internet quiz site.

During my twenty-five years as a corporate consultant, I administered hundreds of assessments and personality profiles—that's a long time to completely understand when it comes to personalities, we have them, and so do dogs. As a matter of fact, our dogs will reflect our personalities—and, sometimes, they'll begin to look like us. Or, we look like them. Either way, our dogs accept themselves as they are, and we can learn a thing or two from them. Some people, as you know, buy a certain vehicle to show off who they are—and, many of us get the breed of dog most like our individual personalities. I did! When I was in Colorado, I spent time outdoors, and I had two, beautiful German shepherds, training them for search and rescue. When my life changed, the dog suiting my current lifestyle is the Boston terrier—the breed is easy to pack and pick up quickly, and it's entertaining while showing a high degree of intelligence.

For me, the breed is exceptional!

So, how do you know which breed is best for you? Simple—research. There are numerous websites to find information about the breed that will suit you best, as well as several quizzes to learn what kind of dog you would be—in other words, given your personality, which dog is most like you?

Lana and I are proof personality quizzes work—after taking a quiz to learn which breed was most like me, it turned out I was a Jack Russell. I get that! Lana was a Boston—I get that, too! Friends say I'm Lana on steroids—well, a Jack Russell terrier is a Boston terrier on steroids.

Here's the description of my personality:

You're a Jack Russell. You're very smart, full of energy, and determined to get what you want. No matter what it is, you eventually get it. You aren't a couch potato—you're full of energy, and never get tired.

Interesting, isn't it? I haven't decided if we choose who we are in the dogs we select, or if we choose who we want to be. Some tell me Dickens, our Boston terrier, wasn't typical for the breed. When we visited our veterinarian, as soon as Dickens sat on the examining table, the vet would lean in for a typical Boston face-washing kiss.

Nothing.

"Well—this isn't your typical Boston," he said during every visit. "Normally, I would have my face being licked clean!"

Not our Dickens. All he really cared about was the certainty that Lana, a few select friends, and I loved him. Few others were significant, and strangers were pretty much ignored unless they could prove themselves useful at playing with one of his many toys.

Lana is just like him. Anyone who knows her well will tell you she's discerning and independent. She treasures her friends, but quality means much more to her than quantity, so she doesn't let others into her circle easily—nor does she require attention or validation from everyone she meets. Just like Dickens. Lana requires only a select group of special friends and family love her even though she has many acquaintances she cares about deeply—her life, however, is full from her core pack.

Me? I used to be a big dog kind of guy. Born into a military family, I was very involved with boy scouts, loving camping and the outdoors. The Scouts suited me, and I learned I tend to step naturally into authoritative, leadership roles. Although my personality has the energy of a Jack Russell, I love and respect the order and authority of the military when it comes to my work. Not so Jack Russell-ish!

Before I met Lana, my choice for dogs was two beautiful 'alpha' German shepherds—Kaizer and Katie, and I referred to them as them 'K2.' They were gorgeous dogs, attracting attention wherever they went, and that was okay with me. Remember when Lana and I met at a corporate conference in Alaska for which I was the keynote speaker, and I shared my love for dogs? Well, when I mentioned my training of K2 for part-time search and rescue, I had no idea of its impact!

That caught Lana's attention!

"If you're as good as you say you are," she commented to me during a break, "can you help me to teach my dog to poop in the rain?"

A challenge, don't you think?

The short story? I taught Dickens to poop in the rain—but, I had to marry his mom to do it!

****

My passion for training is having fun with a purpose, and thinking like a dog. We see elements of ourselves in many breeds and, as I brought Kaizer and Katie into our relationship, it was clear—of the two dogs, I was Kaizer and Lana was Katie. Kaizer loved to 'snoof,' wandering the forest, looking, sniffing, and discovering. He often dropped his ball, forgetting where he left it in his quest for adventure—and, he needed Katie's keen sense for order to help him find it.

Just like Lana and me.

So, what about you? What breed suits you best? Are you a German shepherd? A Boston? A golden retriever? If you're not sure, take a couple of seconds to describe yourself in five words. Then, after you 'get real' by describing yourself, do your research to find a dog breed that most resembles you! There are many fun Internet quizzes to help you discover which breed best describes your personality.

Like Lana, Katie, always our focused girl, knew where everyone was at all times, and went to the park for the sole purpose of chasing her ball. On the rare occasion when she left her ball behind, we knew that, too, was on purpose. Her passion was a green clutch ball and, when it started to wear out, she decided it was time for a new one by continually hiding it until we got the message.

Another example—Lana's sister had a border collie

named Zihna. She was always active, busy, and friendly, as well as accepting and generous. Zihna loved love and there is no such thing as too much attention from her family. Just like Lynne with her kids, there is no such thing as too much communication, attention, or connection with her children or her family—the ever attentive border collie.

Think of your friends and family who have dogs in their lives—are they similar to their dogs? Do you recognize certain, similar traits?

Another interesting thing—have you ever noticed when someone is walking their dog down the street, you feel more comfortable going up to the dog and talking to it—or, about it—to the owner? Dogs are great ice-breakers, offering us the opportunity to ease into a relationship because we know dogs accept each of us as we are.

Right here. Right now.

Usually, if a dog accepts us, there's a good chance the owner will give us the benefit of the doubt, too. We have a plaque in our home—*if our dog doesn't like you, we probably won't either.* It's true—most of the time, if Barclay the Boston opens up and plays well with someone, chances are we will, too.

So, as you wander your city, notice how many homeless people have dogs as their companions. Street smarts at their finest! Stats show when people are questioned about whether they're comfortable approaching a homeless person, they're more likely to approach if the homeless person has a dog—it's easier to engage in some form of conversation.

Lana and I are perfect examples of accepting people as they are, especially if they have a dog. We can't give to everyone, but Lana is hard pressed to walk by someone in need who has a pet by his or her side. She'll buy a sandwich for the mom or dad—maybe both—and, a box of bones for their best friend. Accepting people as they are, however, doesn't mean you have to be like them—we're simply suggesting you meet them before passing judgment.

It just feels right.

****

Relationships are a funny thing—sometimes we fall into them without thinking twice. Other times? Not so much. I suppose there are plenty of reasons why that is, but, I happen to believe if we watch dogs, we can learn a whole bunch about how to foster successful relationships. A dog or pet living with a homeless person has no sense they're homeless—in fact, they probably spend more time with their 'parent' than we do with our pets.

Unlike many relationships, however, dogs don't want you to be perfect—they just want you to be. Can you imagine? Wouldn't it be nice if we could suspend judgment in our relationships just like dogs? By doing so, I think we'd learn each of us is doing our best at 'doing our best.' Chances are if you walk down the street with your pet and were to come across a movie star or a homeless person, your pet's reaction to either of the them would be equal—to them, there is no difference.

Can you say the same for you?

Dickens was raised by Skeeter, our cat. He loved to play, and he was prepared to get along with anyone who had the same mindset. I suspect he probably knew Skeeter was his sister, but he also recognized she was different. Nonetheless, when he had the opportunity to forge relationships with some other cats, he offered them the same chance for friendship as he did Skeeter. Katie and Kaizer, on the other hand, had to be guided into a relationship with Skeeter because they were raised with other shepherds who weren't around cats. That made building a relationship with Skeeter more difficult—for the dogs and the cat!

The point is there's so much to learn from those who are different from us, whether it's in experience, nationality, gender, religion, or age. Lana and I believe it's through our differences we grow and, by confronting those differences, we begin to see who we really are. Do we come with rigid conditions and judgments, or are we accepting and non-judgmental?

Are we capable of total acceptance?

Here's the thing—most dogs will play with anyone who has a toy—so will most children. Why? Because they like to have fun! Who doesn't? And, everyone has the potential to be fun until they prove themselves otherwise. To a dog or child, everyone is a potential new friend—there isn't a preference for ethnicity, gender, color, sexual orientation, religion, or political affiliation, and they play no part in the decision-making process. To a dog or child, though, everyone is a potential new friend. A dog or child is willing to give you everything they have, and they'll love you unconditionally—that's if you'll throw the ball, or take them for a walk.

Such simple needs.

It's the pesky adults who throw a wrench into the works—that's when things begin to change. Think about this—do we teach judgment and prejudice to our children? Do we teach aggression and bad manners to our dogs? Remember, our pets can't use words, but they surely can imitate our actions and thoughts. Just like children, puppies will accept anyone who's nice as their friend—it's only adults who teach differences between all of us. Dogs look at other breeds and see another dog. That's it.

There's no such thing as prejudice.

The truth is when it comes to prejudice, our dogs can teach us a lot, if we're willing to learn—unfortunately, our prejudice blinds us to the talent and gifts each of us carry throughout our lives. When we shut down possibilities before we have a chance to recognize them, we miss out on all the perks!

Don't believe me? Then, I throw down a challenge! Spend time with someone whom you think you don't like. I know, I know—it sounds weird. But, when you take the time and make the effort to learn something about that person, it's a great way to understand him or her. I've never understood how someone can refuse to eat something (within reason), and claim not to like it when they haven't even tasted it!

It's the same thing.

It was Dickens who taught Lana and me that lesson. He loved broccoli, and when we prepared vegetables for a crudité tray, he'd stand on his back legs, leaning on our leg with one front paw. It was the look saying, "Now that's dog food!" He didn't eat what he didn't like, but he considered everything once.

Lana taught him vegetables were good, and she decided they were the healthy treats on which she wanted him to grow up. In fact, vegetables and cheese were the only people food Dickens knew until I came into the picture. Honestly? It didn't occur to me to introduce raw vegetables to Katie and Kaizer—they were meat eating German shepherds!

Unfortunately, my stereotyping taught them what I thought they should be. However, I soon learned I, too, needed to learn to accept others as they are. Ever since I can remember, I had a prejudice toward small dogs—until I met Dickens. The eighty-pound heart inside his fifteen-pound body changed the way I looked at a lot of things.

I can honestly say, when I walked Dickens for the first time on the city streets of Vancouver, B.C., I was embarrassed. I was used to two, one hundred pound German shepherds walking with me—but, my embarrassment turned quickly to admiration when we came to a street crossing. Stopping for the light and waiting for the cross-walk signal, I looked down to see him in a perfect sit at my left knee, looking up at me as if to say, "Hi! This is great, isn't it? I'm having a really good time!"

The point? Just this—he had no idea he wasn't one hundred pounds, and it didn't occur to him I was struggling with my prejudices. They didn't last long, I can tell you that!

Because of Dickens, I smile when I see people carrying their dogs like Barbie dolls. I learned acceptance, and now I understand when I see a short-haired dog wearing a raincoat or snow boots. The old me? I used to scoff at ALL dog apparel. *Clothes are for people, not dogs*, I'd scream to myself! *You'll never see one of my dogs wearing a coat!* Of course, the shepherds didn't need coats—their natural, double coat of hair was enough to keep them warm. It wasn't until the first time I put a raincoat on Dickens's bald little body, I realized I had been stereotyping dogs due to my ignorance and global 'dog generalization.' Because Dickens was so different from anything I previously experienced—and, because of the positive impact he had on my life—my acceptance level broadened, and I now see other people and other animals with more compassion, humility, and acceptance.

Sadly, though, well-intended prejudice of people we love can hinder their ability to experience life. Lana was very protective of Dickens due to his size, and she decided well in advance what he was and was not capable of doing—without giving him the chance to try.

I was guilty of the same thing.

A great example of thinking I knew everything about dogs took place in the forest outside of our home. One day, we headed into the woods with three balls, and a sense of adventure. It was spring and the creek wasn't deep, but it was flowing at a pretty good clip. Katie and Kaizer were up and down the banks, crossing the creek, having a wonderful time. Dickens tended to race along the shore because getting wet and cold wasn't on his list of things to do. In the midst of our fun, I threw Dickens's ball up the creek, and he went flying after it—but, the water was too deep, and we lost it. Or, I should say, I thought we lost it.

Dickens? He was convinced he'd find it, and finding the ball became our search and rescue mission. Fallen trees, deep pockets of water, three dogs, and one man—all determined to win the battle.

Lana headed home to grab my hip waders, calling Dickens to join her, always the cautious parent. I remember vividly as he stood on the top of a log in the middle of the creek looking directly at her. I think it was then he decided to become a 'big' dog—he decided he could do what Katie and Kaizer did, only his way. He was part of the pack, and he would cross the creek back and forth just like they did, only on top of logs versus through cold water. It were as if we could 'hear' him make the decision to become part of the big-dog pack.

Lana set off, returning moments later with gear allowing me to head down the middle of the creek on our mighty adventure.

Too bad I didn't need it!

Dickens found his ball stuck against some sticks far down the creek. He traversed the water, turtled logs, and went everywhere we went, but he did it his way. His ingenuity and desire to accomplish tasks alongside his bigger brother and sister were inspiring! And, to think Lana would have taken him home, thinking he couldn't do it, or she would have carried him, suspecting he wasn't capable.

I probably don't have to tell you that was the last time we saw Dickens as different from the pack.

Of course, there were obvious tasks he couldn't accomplish but, for the most part, he did them his way—and, we allowed him to try instead of deciding about his abilities ahead of time.

We were learning, through our dogs, to accept others as they are.

****

One year after we lost Dickens in September of 2009, we headed to West Vancouver Island with Kaizer, Katie, and

Skeeter to camp for ten days at Tofino—respectively, they were twelve years old, eleven-and-a-half, and seventeen. Skeeter was blissfully unaware cats don't camp and, per our credo to let them try, we didn't tell her. It turned out she had a fabulous time with all of us—safe, sound, and dry in our tent with her food, cow pillow, and kitty litter! Nice digs, don't you think?

Only once during our ten-day camping trip did Lana falter for a moment when I suggested we take Skeeter to the beach with us, so she could see the waves. She immediately thought, *No. Skeeter won't like the beach—she won't like the water.* Still, off we went—all five of us!

Skeeter did think the waves were pretty loud, but as Katie and Kaizer settled down among the drift wood, so did she. We put her on a long leash, and she putzed around on the logs, jumping on and off, finally settling in the warm sand beside her brother and sister. On the way back, Lana faltered once again by picking up Skeeter to carry her back to camp.

Well, as you can imagine, Skeeter wasn't having any of it. She wiggled and squirmed and, finally, on the end of her leash, trotted behind K2 as we headed up the trail. The look on other people's faces as they were coming down the path was priceless—definitely not an every day sight! She trekked about ten minutes before her princess genes kicked in and she sat down, deciding that was enough exercise for one day. It was the clear signal she would happily allow herself to be carried back to camp!

I can tell you example after example of how we learn from our animals, but the upshot is this—after paying closer attention to our little family, I realized I didn't have to surround myself with people who think exactly the way I do. Instead, a neighborhood of shepherds, Bostons, mixed-blood dogs, cats, and birds simply added to the value of diversity,

So, what do you think? How's your judgment, acceptance, righteousness, and prejudice working for you? If it's not contributing, it's contaminating. K2 and Skeeter worked out their differences . . . why can't we?

Lana's sister—the one with the border collie—had the most amazing rule on her small acreage in Oregon where she used to live—*if it has a name, you can't chase it, or eat it.* Imagine living our lives by that rule!

It's all about respect.

Yes, I know it's an idealistic approach—after all, we're a complicated species. Even so, we'll take the simplistic approach, creating a one percent improvement in one hundred people, situations, or beliefs over a one hundred percent change in any one of those.

The bottom line? One mind shift at a time will make our world a better place.

When it comes to unconditional love and knowing there is a story behind each one of us, I would gladly exchange my understanding of myself with that of my dogs. All of us can strive to understand what our dogs already know . . .

Accept others as they are.

Rule #3

Focus on the Positive

*"Your positive action combined with positive thinking
result in success."*
—Shiv Khera

If you're anything like me, there are days when things just aren't going right—pretty sure it happens to all of us. Most times, a word of encouragement from someone sparks us to perform better, or feel like the Energizer bunny. It's at that moment, words of encouragement or kindness become an investment in that person—from the outside in— yielding dividends from the inside out.

So it is with dogs.

Offered at just the right time, a word of encouragement tells them what they should continue to do—conversely, a reprimand can stop a behavior from becoming a bad habit. From that perspective, a reprimand is nothing more than negative encouragement—it's not given to break the dog's spirit, but rather to guide it in the direction we want it to go.

It's the same with people.

Think about your dog—or, dogs—for a second. What do you notice? They watch us continually for a positive or negative reinforcement of their behavior.

Not so different from us, huh?

In *Rule #2, Accept Others as They Are*, I told you I remember walking Dickens for the first time in Vancouver, then coming to a stop. He immediately sat, looking up at me for a reaction and positive reinforcement. I provided what he needed with an emphatic, "Good boy! Good sit!" It was all he needed.

It was all he wanted.

Now, with Barclay, we trained him to do his business when we ask him—it makes going for a car ride much more pleasant to know everyone used the bathroom! There's a special tilt to his head when we ask if he wants to go and, once we're on our walk, we say, "Do your business, Barclay," and he knows what we expect. Sometimes, at the end of his business, he stops for one last leg-up—the BWH (Barclay Was Here)—then looks at us expecting the customary praise.

The point is dogs are always looking for positive reinforcement—just like us.

Think about this—do you notice, more often than not, you give your dog an 'attaboy' easier than you offer it to your partner, spouse, or children? I do. In fact, one of my dog-training techniques is to have owners look for the opportunity to praise their dogs early—what I call 'preemptive praise.' You can do it by watching for behaviors you want to see upon command, then praise them before they do it. For example, when your puppy is getting ready to sit, right before he does you say, "Good SIT!" When your dog is ready to lie down, turns in a circle, and lies down, you say, "Good DOWN!" By implementing that simple technique, you're looking for the behavior you want to reward and praise.

Now, consider performing this exercise with people in your life—can you imagine how relationships would grow and strengthen if you're always looking for things you want to praise or reward? How great would it feel to be noticed for doing something right instead of being in a culture of commenting on what you do wrong?

One thing I know for certain—if you look for bad behavior, or if you believe people are mean, fat, or poorly dressed, etcetera, you'll find it. But, when you believe people are basically kind, that's what you notice because we look to prove ourselves right. Makes sense, doesn't it? Wouldn't it feel better to look for and find the good stuff?

'Good boy' or 'good girl' to your family members may attract a negative reaction, but try watching out for positive behaviors and saying thank you more often, and see what happens. "Thanks for clearing the table, I really appreciate it." Or, "Thanks for putting the dishes away . . ."

When training dogs, I always encourage owners to use positive reinforcement. What does that mean? Comment on well-done deeds. Focus on what's working. Think about this—we all like to be praised rather than punished. The same is true for animals, and that's the theory behind *Focus on the Positive.*

Of course, it's a good bet you probably already know positive reinforcement means giving pleasant or rewarding feedback immediately after someone does something we like. Because of our praise—or, reward—they're more likely to repeat the behavior in the future. It's one of our most powerful tools for shaping or changing behavior—ours, and our dog's!

Here's a good example of what I mean—Dickens loved to play, and he was really good at making it known when and how that was supposed to happen. He also had his own rules, and we had to be smarter than he if we wanted to insert our terms into the game. Like many well-loved dogs, Dickens didn't always do what he was told, and Lana excused his imperfections by saying, "It's his game—therefore, he gets to play it his way." That was her reasoning for why he didn't have to drop the ball on command.

The solution? I knew Dickens loved being praised for being a good boy, so I soon learned a solution to finding a way to play my way. Whenever he would come over with his ball and drop it—in his own good time—I would immediately say, "Good drop, Dickens! Good drop!"

The look on his face was so comical, as if he were startled for being told he was good when he knew he should have dropped it five minutes earlier.

And, so it continued.

I praised him as soon as he dropped the ball, and I reached forward to reinforce the compliment with a pat on the head. So . . . that was a nice thought, but we couldn't begin to get close enough to pat him on the head because as soon as he dropped the ball, he was heading off to get a head start on the next throw!

The next time he came back, we praised him for dropping his ball, he dropped it a minute sooner, then another minute sooner. Eventually, he came close enough to pet. The best part was he'd hang around for a moment to be praised before he took off, waiting for the ball to fly over his head. The other best part was I'm pretty sure both of us were smiling.

The above example is a simple one, but who says positive reinforcement has to be difficult? Since you're reading this book, I assume you love animals—especially your dog. But, what if you tried the same technique on anyone in your life? I guarantee you'll have the same great feeling I did when Dickens stuck around for a well-deserved pat on the head. I know, I know—as a dog trainer, I could have gone about it in a more structured manner, but I wanted to focus on the positive—it's so critically important. By Lana's not wanting to dictate orderly rules to Dickens's game and, by my choosing positive reinforcement, all of us got what we wanted.

Works for me!

If you think positive reinforcement is something you

want to try—at home, work, or anywhere—correct timing is essential. The reward must occur immediately—within seconds—otherwise, the person or dog you're rewarding may not associate it with the proper action. For example, if I have a dog sit, but reward it after it stands up, the dog will think it's being rewarded for standing up. The same thing holds true for kids. If you let too much time elapse before you praise them, you lose the impact of rewarding the good behavior.

Consistency is also essential. It takes at least twenty-one days to change a behavior and replace it with another. So, if you're curious, for the next three weeks try to be as consistent as possible by recognizing, rewarding, and repeating positive reinforcement. I'll bet you're gonna love it!

Anyone (yes—that means you!) can change an office environment, family dynamic, department culture, or even an entire organization by using the positive reinforcement technique. The best part is the technique isn't difficult—a kind, appreciative word is all it takes. And, maybe a pat on the head . . . although, your kids might think you're a weirdo!

Remember to keep your positive reinforcement simple, understandable, and honest. If the process is too complicated or tedious, the attention you're giving will be diluted. Not only that, if the recognition isn't sincere, your efforts will have an opposite effect.

One other thing—not everyone likes to be rewarded or reinforced the same way. Therefore, it's important to understand what type of person he or she is, then reward accordingly. It's the same with dogs—many are driven by the desire for food. Katie and Kaizer were like that, but Dickens didn't have a high food drive. He and Barclay are driven by fun. Games! A good time!

Dickens's loved chasing a ball—an activity showing a high prey drive. He was so smart, he would invent a game, play it, and win—he created his own positive reinforcement! Not only that, he'd invent the game, teach it to us, then give us positive reinforcement for playing it with him. It gave me pause, though—I wasn't sure, who was training who (I wish you could see me smiling at the memory!)

One of Dickens's favorite things to do was gently chew on a small, green rubber ball, cradled in my hand. He would lie down, use his paw to turn over my arm, place his paw firmly over my wrist so I couldn't' move my hand, place the ball in my palm, and begin to chew. Unfortunately, some guests didn't know the game and, on more than one occasion, Dickens landed beside them on the couch and flipped their arm, tossing what was in their hand (often a glass of wine), so his ball would fit neatly in their palm. It happened so fast, they didn't know what happened to them, or their drink!

Lana and I long since learned—the hard way—we could head off impending disaster by seating people in chairs versus on the couch, but, sometimes, we missed, too. But, that was okay—we were more impressed with his ability to teach others how to play his game than we were bothered by the occasional miscalculation and subsequent mess. We chose to focus on his brilliance—which was positive—versus his destruction.

When you think about it, Dickens had a lot of talent and perseverance to teach his game to guests—the game of holding the ball for him so he could chew it. Eventually, most of our guests learned how to do it right and, once they got it, he received a lot of praise and positive reinforcement for being such a smart boy!

Now, think about what behavior you don't want, whether it's by people or dogs. Knowing what you don't want is just as important as knowing what you do want when it comes to focusing on the positive. You will set up someone for success instead of failure by clearly asking for what you want.

When it comes to dog training, it's imperative you think like a dog. If our dog—or, loved one—tilts their head sideways, then, maybe, we need to do a better job of making our expectations understood. It works the same for dogs as people—if we need to create understanding, then we should clearly share what we expect.

****

A more frequent example of positive reinforcement and reward for both of us is whenever we hear the shower stop, we grab a towel off the rack and hand it to the other person to stay warm in the shower as they dry off.

On one occasion when Lana's mom was visiting, we noticed Dickens standing in the hallway as we got ready for bed. It was a new behavior, and we could only think something changed. "What's going on," we asked Dickens, then Mom. She informed us while we were gone and she was babysitting Dickens, she threw his fluffy blanket into the dryer just before he went to bed. It took only one time for Dickens to focus on this positive new pattern and, from then on, every night during the winter, he would stand in the hall in front of his crate, waiting patiently for the dryer to stop, and the warm blanket to be tucked into his bed.

That was it—a new, positive ritual.

I know it may sound silly to some, but one thing I've learned throughout my experience with dogs, especially Dickens—kind gestures go a long way to help us focus on the positive.

Giving and receiving.

Let's build relationship just like our dogs . . .

When raising pets, we made some foolish and regretful mistakes along the way, and I wish we would've done things differently. Yet, when I think back, our pets didn't appear to think any less of Lana and me—their bank of love continues to fill with every pat on the head, or toss of a ball. Their love is in the present, unconditional and, in all ways, accepting.

Let's face it—we can drive ourselves crazy focusing on the past, or on behaviors over which we have no control, or can't undo. If, in our daily lives, we focus on the positive, there would be no room for gossip or verbal abuse. You know the old saying—*if you don't have something good to say, don't say anything at all.* Somewhere along the way, I believe, we forgot such an important rule.

****

For many reasons, pets hold a special place in our lives and hearts that's difficult to comprehend—maybe it's their gift of unconditional love that cements the relationship. Maybe it's their ability to hold a confidence, and share in our most special memories. I don't profess to know, but I know their love for us is extraordinary.

When Lana and I reminisce, we tend to focus on how great the dogs were, and how proud we were of their behavior. When Dickens was a puppy, Lana's best friend remembers thinking, *this is a devil dog, and you're in for some real challenges.* I guess Dickens had quite the little Boston terrorist temper, and, if Lana picked him up in the middle of doing something, disturbing his concentration, he would go bonkers!

To this day, Lana has very little recollection of that happening. Our memories of Dickens are of the great things he did—we feel the same about Katie, Kaizer and Skeeter, Barclay, and Cheddar. We choose to remember all that is good, and it's our pattern—and, rule—to *focus on the positive.* How we think of our animals is a good benchmark for how we think of people. You and I know life isn't all roses, and we have some work to do when it comes to focusing and commenting on negative human behaviors. Maybe we need to love unconditionally more, live in the moment more, and *build relationships like a dog.*

We're continually taking time to praise our pets, telling them how great they are. We have fun looking in their faces, scuffing around their ears with a smile on our faces saying, "You're the best dog I've seen today!" Without question, they know they're loved every day! Lana smiles every time she recounts the story she calls *Katie's Story . . .*

When Lana and I first got together, we lived in a little hobbit house in Vancouver with lots of doors, and hardwood floors throughout—perfect for our four-legged family. We loved having the dogs on their beds in the kitchen and, on one particular night as Lana finished the dishes, she heard behind her, "You know—you really are the most beautiful girl!" Having had a long day at work, the compliment was exactly what she needed. Well, she turned to thank me for the loving compliment, then stopped mid-sentence, realizing I was staring directly at Katie. My compliment was for the dog, not her!

Focusing on the positive, we still laugh about it today, but it made me realize I give out strong compliments to our pets, yet I assume Lana knows how beautiful she is to me. Enough said.

My question to you is . . . are you dishing out such affirmations to your family and friends? It's easy to say such things to our pets, but, if you're saying them to friends, colleagues, and family . . . well done!

Rule # 4

Forgive and Forget

"The first step in forgiveness is the willingness to forgive"

—*Marianne Williamson*

It says in the Good Book, "Forget the former things, do not dwell on the past."

There are no truer words.

Dogs will correct their offspring in the moment, and the lesson is taught, learned, and remembered—for life. They don't remember the past, but learn from it so they can be better in the future. A great lesson, don't you think? Too often, we remember and remind loved ones of their faults, never letting go of the past, thereby robbing them—and, ourselves—of a positive future.

Since dogs live in the moment, they either speak up, or forever hold their peace. They have an amazing ability to forgive us almost instantly for our mistakes—we're the ones who hold grudges. As humans, we often bring up a mistake time and time again—and, for some reason, we have a more difficult time letting go. If you're conscious of how dogs think, you'll know you can't refer to a past mistake, and expect it to make much sense to them. The same thing holds true for a grudge—carrying a grudge, and expecting them to know why you're miffed doesn't make sense.

When a mother is raising a litter of pups and she sees one of the litter doing something wrong, she disciplines them in that moment, then lets it go. Mistakes made in the past are in the past, and the pups either learn from the discipline they received, or not. In the moment, they're disciplined, taught, and they learn. And, that's *Rule #4—Forgive and Forget*. Think about that! Communicating in the moment, then letting it go forever? What a concept!

We have so much to learn from our pets, don't we?

You know it's our nature to be attracted to pleasure, and shy away from pain. Or, more important, to avoid physical pain, if we can. We remember pain associated with the errors of our ways, but, as time passes, sometimes we forget and repeat our mistakes. Not so with dogs—I believe they're ahead of the game when it comes to learning. They'll test us, push us and, sometimes, will us to show them the boundaries—but, once they learn where those lines are, they're pretty good at remembering what they can do. Or, not.

Let me share a story about Dickens—a story Lana recalls with a smile. She was living in Calgary and, on one sunny Saturday, she was busy cleaning her house. Dickens was about four years old, and he, too, wanted to be busy—playing with Lana. He had tons of toys, and Lana would throw his ball once in a while, but, there were chores to do, and she didn't throw the ball nearly enough for his liking. As part of her cleaning, Lana took the bed's duvet to the laundromat, washed it, dried it, came home, and put it back on the bed—one chore down, another one to go.

Dickens didn't see it that way.

Strong-minded and doing his best to get her attention, he pushed the limits. A few minutes after making the bed, Lana noticed a large, wet, pee area on the duvet cover. Oh, Dickens snagged her attention, alright! She hadn't caught him doing it, but, since she didn't pee on the bed, she had a good idea about the culprit. He looked a bit guilty and suspected he was in trouble, but, since the event already occurred and she hadn't caught him in the act, she didn't discipline him with as much enthusiasm as if she saw him doing the deed.

Back to the laundromat.

But, that was okay with Dickens. He was a pretty happy guy—he and Lana were together, AND he was going for another car ride.

Life was good.

They returned home an hour later, and Lana set to making the bed—again—and, continuing with her chores. Five minutes later—noticing it seemed awfully quiet in the bedroom—she peeked around the corner to see Dickens squatting in the middle of the duvet, peeing! Nooooooo! This time he was caught in the act, and the discipline was swift and sure!

Now, there's a proper way to discipline dogs that's effective and meaningful—domination. Lana grabbed Dickens by his little jowls, held his face in front of hers, and stared into his eyes telling him he was a bad dog, and saying

NO! She kept that pose until HE turned his eyes away from her—position and discipline established, learning noted, and logged.

It was all that needed to happen.

There was no pouting or glaring at Dickens for the next two hours, and he didn't have to sit in the corner. He was disciplined in the moment, Lana forgot about it, and all was forgiven. Back they went back to the laundromat, washed the duvet—again—came home, and remade the bed. No pee-stained duvet was ever seen again.

Often, we see humans discipline animals and each other in the moment, but carry a grudge or anger for hours —maybe days. What good does that do except make you feel miserable? Say your peace, make your point, and let it go! It's done! Over!

But, you and I know forgiveness isn't that easy—it isn't a quick fix. There are complicated, contributing factors involved in the act of forgiveness, and it's our nature to hold onto the hurt so we can justify our feelings of anger, mistrust, and resentment.

You get the idea.

But, I think dogs have known the secret to forgiveness since creation—loyalty. If you ask anyone to list the attributes of their dogs, most people will include loyalty—in fact, dogs are so loyal, they seem to overlook any faults or missteps we show them.

In customer service, the ultimate relationship between business and customer is loyalty, and I believe the level of loyalty is directly proportional to the level of service received. And, from loyalty comes forgiveness—the more you build a relationship with someone or a service, it's likely you'll show forgiveness should something go wrong.

Levels of forgiveness exist in the dog world, as well. When I was working with Waterton Canyon Kennels in Littleton, Colorado, breeding, raising, and training German shepherds, we had a structured placement process. Part of the process for the dogs was an eight-point personality drive test given to each dog on the forty-ninth day—placement day. The personality test covered several drives, one of which was a drive for forgiveness. Our intent was to match the dog's personality to the potential owner's situation and temperament.

The forgiveness drive was important to placing the dog in the right situation, and we wanted to place a dog with a high forgiveness drive in situations involving children, older people, those physically challenged, or any situation where something unexpected may happen to the dog, physically. The reaction to the event had to be a stable emotional response—the dog's reaction returning to the emotional level BEFORE the event. The measurement was the shorter time between unexpected physical pain and emotional forgiveness behavior.

During Katie's time with me, she raised two litters, totaling eighteen pups, four of which became therapy dogs— the epitome of emotional stability supported by the capacity to forgive. That was when my awareness to 'think like a dog' became part of my behavior DNA—it was to become my 'Camelot on the hill' when it came to *building relationships like a dog*.

In dogs—humans, too—there's a scale as to how fast the animal forgives an owner for pain, or mistakes. If we watch dogs posture when asking for forgiveness, the signs are obvious—they'll lower their bodies to the ground, expose their vital organs (bellies) and throats to the dominant dog, and shower them with kisses by licking the lips of the dominant dog.

When our pets ask for our forgiveness, it seems easier to

forgive them than it is to forgive family or friends. At least, that's the way it was for me when I was younger—it was easy to apologize to my pets for a behavior or mistake I made with them. I remember trying to practice that same humility with my boys, apologizing when needed, and forgiving them for things they said, or did.

Dogs tend to associate pain with a moment in time while remembering the experience for a while, but, they're quick to reestablish trust and rebuild confidence. I believe it's possible because they can forgive.

By admiring our pets' ability to forgive us, I was inspired to look at myself in the mirror. If I can't forgive, is it a choice? Can I forgive? Am I willing to forgive? Do I hang on to my anger or displeasure, withholding forgiveness of myself and others? It's no secret forgiving someone else is sometimes easier than forgiving ourselves—one is public, the other, private. When it comes to forgiveness, we must ask ourselves if we can't forgive, how is it serving us? There's the difference—I don't imagine dogs think about forgiving themselves.

They just live in the moment, and move on.

Unlike people who hold grudges and harbor negative

feelings from a bad experience, dogs don't hold grudges. I used to get so mad at Katie—when we left the garbage bag on the back deck occasionally, she would tear into it to get to the chicken bones.

In that instance, there were three issues at work: one, I needed to teach her in the moment, and stop the behavior. Two, I needed to forgive her quicker after she'd been disciplined since I held a grudge. Third, I should've put the garbage in a secure can! In fact, it was Lana who reminded me I was the one attracting the bad behavior by placing the garbage there in the first place. I would get so mad at Katie, I stormed around the house punishing her—and, anyone else who was around—with a stern look, being miserable. She got it the first time, and probably had no idea as the day passed why I was in such a bad mood.

When we make a mistake, or hurt them intentionally or unintentionally, they forgive us quickly. If it's something such as getting stepped on, they remember and learn they need to keep out of our way to avoid being stepped on again— but, they certainly don't know how to hold a grudge. I'm not convinced Katie could understand my anger was based on something she did hours earlier. Thinking about it now, I feel badly I missed out on that time when we could have been connecting with each other. Regardless, as soon as I snapped out of my immaturity, I was forgiven. *Thank you for the lesson, Katie-girl—I'm much better at this rule with Barclay and Cheddar!*

Everybody starts fresh every day with dogs and, sometimes, forgiving isn't the same as forgetting. For example, when Katie and Kaizer were senior citizen dogs, we carried a ramp in the back of our truck to allow them to come and go without jumping in or out. One day, I put the ramp up to the tailgate on an angle for easier access, and went over to the gate to get K2.

Before I could stop them, the two of them were off to the races. As Katie ran up the ramp, it tipped over on its side. Kaizer, who was right behind her, hit the ramp as it was tipping, catching it right in his chest. It stopped him dead in his tracks, and everyone on the block could hear his cries. I felt terrible and, although we trained them to wait until I was at the ramp, in their excitement, they didn't.

Kaizer never forgot that painful lesson, and was forever cautious approaching the ramp. I still feel badly about my error, even though he probably didn't associate me with his pain—he probably associated me as the person trying to comfort him. The good news is self-forgiveness or forgiveness of others can lessen the grip on the negative, helping us focus on more positive aspects of our lives.

It's another lesson we can learn from our dogs—they forgive and forget so well.

After the 'incident,' Kaizer still wanted to go for a ride in the truck, but he waited for me to give him permission before he stepped onto the ramp. Abused dogs that have been injured seem to bounce back and thrive, and I think it's because they continue to naturally forgive, and hope for the best. I think a part them can't believe we did something to them on purpose. What great, hopeful expectations they have for us!

Lana sometimes shares a metaphor about thinking before we act or speak. Most of us have betrayed someone, spread gossip, or hurt someone we love. When we say or do something hurtful, it's like hammering a nail into a board. We can apologize, buy flowers, or do any number of things to say we're sorry—in a sense, pulling the nails out of the board, but the holes remain. Over time, the holes fill in, and the pain from the hurt fades. Unlike dogs, I know we're still developing the quickness to completely forgive.

If we can forgive, then, like dogs, we can stop counting. I'm convinced, dogs don't count—they don't count how many times we visit, how many times we call. It's called unconditional acceptance and love. They teach us by doing things because they want to, and because it feels good—not because they expect something in return.

   Dogs give their love as a gift—not an obligation.

Rule #5

Run with the Right Pack

"The moment you accept responsibility for EVERYTHING in your life is the moment you gain the power to change ANYTHING in your life."

—Hal Elrod

Motivational speaker, Jim Rohn, said, "We are the average of the five people with whom we spend the most time . . ." I believe that to be true because it relates to the law of averages, the theory being the result of any given situation will be the average of all outcomes. When it comes to the wisdom of the crowd, results become more accurate.

Dogs are pack animals, and so are we. In the wild, you will rarely—if ever—see a coyote or wolf on its own and, if you do, chances are its pack is nearby. They function best as a group, choose their teams well, and they live by a set of rules ensuring survival.

The same can be said of us.

When we choose a bad pack, we may not thrive, or survive.

Think about the Internet for a second—online dating and matchmaking companies are plentiful as people try to match themselves with someone who will bring them fulfillment and satisfaction. Why? Because life is about relationships—how we live, build, and sustain them.

When we run with the right pack, we can weather the worst crises, and share the best experiences. Support and mastermind groups now dot the business landscape, a perfect example of how we flourish when part of a selected pack. Hobbies and interests attract groups of people by age, profession, and gender—the list goes on. Social media often precludes face-to-face conversations, and many people type better than they talk. Social networking and media promote cyber groups, but, they're packs, nonetheless.

Lana and I agree with Rohn—you're the average of the five people with whom you spend most of your time. Who are your work colleagues and friends you invite over for dinner? Who do you talk to most throughout the day?

When my sons were growing up and bringing new friends into their lives, I asked, "Who's influencing who?" If you're a parent, you probably know exactly what I'm talking about—asking that question was my way of getting them to think about who was in their pack. Not only that, I wanted my boys to think about the identity they were developing as a result of the friends in their circles. My sister, Bernie, used to say, "Show me who your friends are, and I'll tell you what kind of person you are." Translation? If things aren't going the way you want them to, look around. See who you're associating with, and ask yourself if they're contributing to your growth, or contaminating it.

Dogs are the original pack animals, automatically establishing alpha male and females to have order in their society. The reason dogs are man's best friend is because of the partnership developed as we domesticated them into our lives. Pack behavior is natural and, in my dog training when I see a dog with behavior problems, it's frequently due to the dog's not knowing its number, or where it fits in the pack.

I suspect the same could be said of many children. Do they think they're alpha in the pack? Many of them certainly behave as if they're the alpha family member. If you've ever seen a puppy assert his authority to his mom or dad, you'll know what I mean. Their place in the pack is swiftly redefined, and order is reestablished on the spot. When we introduce a puppy into our homes, like a child, it will try to establish itself as the alpha in the family. It should, however, be at the back of the pack, or own the last number in the group—until there's another addition. Then it moves up in the order.

Often, as singles, we bring dogs into our lives for company—that makes us their only pack. Since they have none of their own, it's important to ensure you teach them the rules—specifically, their position. Like children, they count on us to teach them their place.

As pack animals, most dogs will try to establish themselves as alpha if there's an opportunity. Once a dog learns it's place and knows what's expected, it becomes a healthy member of the larger group. They vie for the top spot, but many thrive further down the ladder because all animals crave direction, order, and leadership until they learn enough to step into a leadership role.

It's an interesting concept when we apply dog ethology—the study of dog pack behavior—to our own family structure. Honestly—what number are you in your pack? What about your children, or other pets? Where do they rank? Alpha dogs aren't friends to the pack—they're the leaders and, as such, are afforded respect and obedience. If you're a mom or dad, it's something to consider as you raise your children. Are you their friend, or are you their teacher and ultimate pack leader as they learn their ways in the world? Are you responsible TO them, or responsible FOR them?

Interesting difference, isn't it?

Dogs also have a way of sorting out their own problems to establish order in their world—unless we get involved. My brother, Gerard, has a boxer-Australian shepherd mix with a little whippet thrown in. Since we aren't sure about her life, what her beginning was, or what her original pack looked like, it's interesting to watch Suzie learn her place through spending time with other dogs, my brother, and his wife. She's a wonderful, happy, agile, nimble, and energetic dog—the perfect companion for Gerard and Brenda. They're a complete, happy, family and, because she's a big part of their lives, Suzie is now invited on most excellent adventures. She fits perfectly into their pack as number three, and accepts she doesn't have the worries nor the status an alpha position carries.

Just like with people, there are rules to the pack that make for a smooth, functioning unit, and they demand order for balance and harmony. One time, Gerard and I went camping with Suzie and K2. Katie and Kaizer grew up in the outdoors since I used to work with Boy Scouts, and our family did a lot of camping, as well—not to mention search and rescue work for which they were trained.

So, when we were camping that first day, Suzie was running through the camp, bouncing off the rocks, wheeling down the paths, going nuts. My dogs? They laid around, watching Gerard and me from the back of the truck. Sometimes, while Suzie was bouncing around, they watched from a quiet place around the fire.

Why do I mention it? Well, for the Boy Scouts, one of the cardinal sins is to run through camp or among the tents. If you do, someone will trip and get hurt, or equipment will get damaged. The cardinal rule? NO RUNNING THROUGH THE CAMPSITE!

As the evening wore on, Kaizer and Katie thought it time to teach Suzie the camping rule, both nipping her as she went shooting by.

Problem solved.

From that moment, she took her time walking, a noticeable difference in her behavior.

The pack taught her what she needed to know.

****

Just like the camping experience, when it comes to *building relationships like a dog* in the workplace or at home, there are appropriate and inappropriate behaviors given the time, task, person, or situation. There's a time to have fun, play, use our outside voices, or sit quietly. Our credibility and—in the case of animals, survival—is built on our emotional intelligence to read a situation, then act accordingly. In most instances, when our behavior is credible or appropriate, we will prosper in everything we do.

When our behavior is inappropriate, others can sense and react in ways impeding our advancement or productivity. Dogs, however, will often step in to correct inappropriate behavior to ensure their pack is controlled and safe. Will we speak up to friends and family to correct inappropriate or annoying behavior? Are we willing to hold our pack accountable, or do we cast a blind eye for fear of conflict? You and I know credibility is built on behavior, and people must behave appropriately.

I wonder—are we honest with our friends and family?

****

Katie and Kaizer were working dogs, and they loved their clutch balls because it meant they were going to the park. Once they took care of business, checked the perimeter, made sure other dogs in THEIR park were behaving, and looked for any squirrels needing to know their place—once all was secure, they could eat grass, and relax. With Dickens and, now, Barclay (maybe it's a breed thing), although the terrier in him is bold and brave, he seems to know he's small. When on a leash, he doesn't meet other dogs well. Maybe he feels he's protecting us, or he's extra brave because they think we're protecting him—either way, he seems to want to intimidate the other dog as a form of self-preservation. We solved the issue by bringing play into the mix, and removing restrictions (i.e. the leash). It made sense—everyone meets well when a game is taking place, and it instantly diffuses a face-to-face stand off.

But, individual breeds are different, their personalities as diverse as you can imagine. For instance, take the task of changing a light bulb . . .

• Golden Retriever: *The sun is shining, the day is young, we have our whole lives ahead of us—and, you're inside worrying about a stupid, burned out bulb?*

• Border Collie: *I can do it! Then, I'll replace any wiring that's not up to code.*

• Dachshund: *You know I can't reach that stupid lamp!*

• Rottweiler: *Make me.*

• Boxer: *Who cares? I can still play with my squeaky toys*

in the dark.

• Lab: *Oh, me, me!!!!! Pleeeeeeeeeze let me change the light bulb! Can I? Can I? Huh? Huh? Huh? Can I? Pleeeeeeeeeze, please, please, please!*

• German Shepherd: *I'll change it as soon as I've led these people from the dark, check to make sure I haven't missed anyone, and make just one more perimeter patrol to make sure no one has tried to take advantage of the situation.*

• Jack Russell Terrier: *I'll just pop it in while I'm bouncing off the walls and furniture.*

• Old English Sheep Dog: *Light bulb? I'm sorry, but I don't see a light bulb!*

• Cocker Spaniel: *Why change it?*

• Chihuahua: *Yo no quiero Taco Bulb.* Or . . . *We don't need no stinkin' light bulb.*

• Greyhound: *It isn't moving. Who cares?*

• Australian Shepherd: *First, I'll put all the light bulbs in a little circle . . .*

Not sure it gets any better than that!

****

When we hear the saying 'iron sharpens iron,' it refers to like mindedness intellect, or two solid entities coming together to improve the other. Or, great minds thinking alike. Take German shepherds—they're used for police work because their temperament and constitution make them great dogs for what police departments need.

Conversely, Boston terriers—Dickens and Barclay—are the engineers of the dog world, and they're very different from shepherds. Their purpose is to design fun, have fun, solve puzzles, and share that learning and fun with others. It was remarkable to see Dickens, Katie, and Kaizer develop into a pack and, when we were out in the woods, Dickens was right there with them, knowing his place behind K2. However, his purpose was very different than theirs.

Moving from Florida to Vancouver is a perfect example— remember I said we had to leave K2 at my sister-in-law's place in Oregon until Lana and I found a home in Vancouver that would take three dogs, and a cat? Well, K2 lived with Lynne for several months, and they knew their place in her pack.

Having found a home in Vancouver, we packed up Dickens and Skeeter and traveled to Oregon to collect our family. Well, we arrived, and carried our belongings through the garage into the house. Of course, Dickens—who had been to Lynne's on numerous occasions—went through the garage, and up the stairs to go into the house. *Oh, no, you don't*, Kaizer thought. *No one from this pack goes into the house except the alphas!* So, as Dickens went up the stairs to go in, Kaizer grabbed him by the head, turned around, and deposited him on the garage floor. *Pack rules, Buddy—not Boston rules. Dogs aren't allowed in the house!*

We were stunned. For two reasons, really—first, it's disconcerting to see a huge German shepherd with a little Boston terrier in its mouth and, second, to see pack rules in full view, based on law and order. You can imagine K2's surprise when, after some discussion and coaxing, that little Boston was allowed in the house.

Seeing that, I didn't go inside right away, staying outside respecting the pack's rules, taking time to explain size matters. When we moved into the house in Vancouver, as the pack learned their rules, Katie and Kaizer were welcomed into the house. However, unlike Dickens and Skeeter, they weren't allowed on the furniture, or beds.

So, how do you know if you're in a pack? One way is nicknames—they're inside recognitions that come with a special knowledge of a person. A good example is Jesse and Frank James, known as the James Gang (I can almost see the puzzled looks on your faces!) Okay—allow me to explain . . .

Lana and Lynne grew up with horses and, when they were kids, they pretended they were Jesse and Frank James. As they grew into adults, they never changed those names— in moments of sister intimacy, they still refer to each other as Jesse and Frank. One summer, while we were sitting around, they decided those closest to them were welcome to join the 'gang,' and I was honored to be invited and given a nickname—Buck. Being welcomed into the inner folds of any family or, in this case the James Gang, is a special feeling. Recently, Lana's mom—who didn't ride horses—at age seventy-nine became the most recent member as Little Joe! How fun to recognize we're never too old to play!

Nicknames are personal, and they're important. Military pilots are given nicknames to signify they're accepted and part of the squadron. Nicknames show us we're in the inner circle of acceptance. Part of a gang. Part of a pack. We usually give nicknames to those we love and, often, those names fall on our pets.

No further explanation needed.

We called Dickens, 'Monk,' Kaizer was 'Mizer' or 'Sausage,' and Katie was 'Katie Lady.' Not to mention 'Skeeter Beet.' Nicknames show others we're within the inner circle of familiarity, and we're personal with them.

Terms of endearment cover the walls of our lives when it comes to our friends, family, and pets. Those nicknames are like verbal touches—gentle and soft.

****

How to behave within a pack is critical to our success, whether within a family, political party, or company. Businesses are now facing a dilemma regarding how to transfer knowledge to the younger workforce coming into boardrooms, and onto shop floors. To ensure future success of their company, they create mentor programs whereby seasoned faculty guide new talent toward a corporate future that's sustainable and healthy.

Understanding differences in styles and approaches brings great wealth to companies and, today, learning is an important factor for success—personally, and professionally. Just like in a dog pack where different goals call for different roles, we must surround ourselves with people who support who we are, yet are different enough to allow us to learn from them.

That's a good thing—not everyone is alike. Searching for and understanding differences in each person—as well as embracing the opportunities to learn from those differences—is something we recognize in dogs and the workplace. Some dogs lie around while others may run for a living. Others can be entertainers—the important thing to remember is whatever the style or purpose, it must contribute to and provide support for the success of the larger group.

In the end, people will always digress into basic, wildlife pack behavior. We only need to look at the common house dog (or, their wolf ancestors) to view the different personality types, and the best blends of teams or packs.

It's understandable why people might say they'd want a team of personalities just like themselves. However, having a mix of personalities creates balance if there are clear roles within the pack to avoid confusion or contention.

Whew! *Rule #5—Run with the Right Pack* is an important rule, and I think it underscores how important running with the right pack is to your life. Your friends' lives. Your family's lives. So, I'll wind it up with this—take stock of your relationships, and ask yourself if your pack is contributing to your development. Then ask if you're providing an important role to the development of others. Finally, if the adage, *you are the average of the people with whom we spend the most time* is true, are you satisfied being the average of your pack? If not, then make a change.

It's all about running with the right pack . . .

Rule #6

"Intention is one of the most powerful forces there is. What you mean when you do a thing will always determine the outcome. The law creates the world."

—*Brenna Yovanoff, The Replacement*

I suspect all dogs are masters of communication—their greatest challenge is our ability to understand what they're saying! I believe their intent is pure, although, sometimes, their communication strategies may not be well thought out.

When it comes to people, we're more complex, and it boils down to only one of two purposes for what we say, think, and do—we contribute to or contaminate any conversation or interaction. So, how do you distinguish between the two?

Know your intent.

By following that simple rule, you can move ahead with complete and open communication, and not be blindsided by the result.

When Cheddar or Barclay want something, intent through their messaging is loud and clear. Barclay is always eager for a car ride, but, if we head out the door with him and he won't jump in, he's telling us he has to do his business first. It took us a couple of times to understand his intent because we were certain he wasn't declining a car ride. Obviously, he couldn't say anything, so it was up to us to think like a dog to understand his intent. With our two-legged friends it's a little easier—we ask questions to validate reasons for saying or doing something. With Barclay, he tilts his head a certain way when we hit the mark—we just need to ask questions more often, as well as be patient enough to listen to his answer.

Our animals communicate as clearly as possible. If they don't want to be touched, they may bite—or, if permitted, leave the area. If they want to play, they usually grab a toy and start barking, or do something to get our attention. You know when your brain feels fried after a long week of work? The same happens to me—but, when Barclay sits in front of me with a ball in his mouth, no matter how tired I am, I still get the message he wants to head outside for a game of fetch.

He communicates his intent, and I understand.

But, what about when they're destructive? What about when they chew the leg of the couch, or tear the stuffing out of your favorite chair? Again, they're trying to show you something—maybe, they're bored. Or, unhappy. Or, it may be something as simple as growing. When Dickens was teething, he used to chew everything because it eased gum pain—his intent wasn't to be destructive. By chewing the corner of the wall in the kitchen and eating the corners off of his carry crate, he got Lana's attention, and she helped find solutions to his problem. I doubt his thinking was complex, but, through Lana's easing his pain, he also learned to go to her for support when he experienced any kind of discomfort.

The main thing is we, as leaders of their pack, have to pay attention to what they're saying—and, we have to figure out their intent. Once that communication happens, it's a glorious day! You're happy! Your dog is happy! All is right with the world!

I know—I'm being dramatic. But, it's true!

Just remember—listen to your pets. They'll tell you everything you need to know!

****

I can hear it now—*what the heck does knowing your dog's intent have to do with building relationships like a dog?* Well, consider the people who are important in your life— when you have a difference of opinion with one of them, there are usually a few different responses you can choose to elevate or deteriorate the conversation. First, you can fly off the handle, get angry, and stomp from the room—but, I gotta tell you, that usually doesn't work too well if you're interested in maintaining a healthy relationship.

Second? You can ignore the difference of opinion, sweeping it under the rug, refusing to deal with or confront it—but, that doesn't sound like a healthy way to go, either. All that will achieve is allowing the situation to fester, and neither one of you will be happy!

Third—figure out your intent. Will your comments or how you present information to each other contribute to your relationship, or contaminate it? By consciously wanting to keep our relationship healthy and growing, when Lana and I find ourselves facing a difference of opinion or a sensitive issue, that's the first thing we figure out. And, we do that *before* we express our opinions.

The same applies in business, and make no mistake—knowing your intent is critical before launching into a heated discussion, or into a respectful learning experience. If your intent is to contribute to the conversation, then positive conversation loops will occur, and you'll end with a good result. It's really that simple—the choice you make will dictate the outcome. You, and only you, choose your thoughts, feelings, and actions—whatever your choice, it will impact everything and everyone around you.

It's all about emotional intelligence.

****

Okay—back to our pets. The best thing I can tell you is 'watch, and learn.' It doesn't make any difference if your pet is a dog or cat, or some other fabulous critter—you have the opportunity to communicate by paying attention to their behavior.

A perfect example is Cheddar—that kitty knows what he wants, when he wants it, and he never hesitates to let us know what he's thinking! We're convinced he's totally brilliant and can tell time—at 7:00, 12:00, 5:00, and 10:00 he makes his intentions known. He'll sound off in the most vocal way he knows and, if that doesn't work, he'll beg by flopping on his back with his legs in the air (we call it the 'Cheddar cheese roll.') If that doesn't get our attention, he'll jump up on the counters, proceeding to the highest levels of anything in the house. Top of the cupboards. Top of the hutch. Anything. All to snag our attention!

Then, at eight o'clock in the evening, there's no misinterpreting our orange kitty's behavior—he wants to go for a walk with his brother. You know how cats will 'snake' around your feet? Well, he does that. Or, he'll sit by the closet where his leash lives, play with our shoes, or sit in front of the door, crying piteously (I thought I was dramatic!)

Of course, Barclay's a big help—he bands with his brother, standing directly in front us, staring, and letting out the occasional whine. Yep—their intent is clear. They want to walk. We know exactly what they want, and we can confirm it by taking them for a stroll, or ignoring them (that almost never happens!) Either way, their intent was well communicated and, nine times out of ten, we're off for a walk.

It's the intent that counts.

When you ask 'what's my intent' and you make a choice to contribute to a relationship, behaviors such as honesty, friendliness, and active listening (I'm sure you can think of a million things) are examples of building your relationships. Don't forget mirroring emotions and dialogue, accepting differences, and thinking of win-win solutions—they're also examples of building relationships.

So—what happens if you choose to skip knowing your intent? It's pretty simple, really—there's a greater chance of contaminating the relationship by being sarcastic. Ignoring someone. Scowling. How can you maintain a healthy, positive relationship with those responses? How can they be good for any relationship?

I think you'll agree—they can't.

By asking 'what is my intent' before you speak, you'll be in the driver's seat when it comes to successful relationships. Many irretrievable, broken, and dysfunctional relationships— office, included—are a result of not considering your intent before you speak.

One more thing—we believe honesty is critical for a successful relationship. Now, I completely understand some of you may be thinking, *If I were to say what I mean, I'd blast the daylights out of somebody!* Not good. However, that may be what you think, but what's the result you want from your interaction? Hopefully, your intent is good, and that blast of honesty would become a puff of good intentions if you make your point with kindness and honesty. Most people want the truth rather than be told a lie, but, if it's a criticism, deliver it with consideration. Deliver it with kindness. Deliver it with caring. Do that, and you'll have the best of all worlds!

As you know, this book is about building relationships like a dog—our four-legged friends want to please and spend time with us. Why? Because it makes them feel good. Their actions speak louder than words, and they're filled with good intentions.

That makes us feel good.

I'll close *Rule #6—Know Your Intent* with this—there are no double standards with animals. They act the way they feel, they're honest in their communication, and they're as clear as they know how to be with their intent.

Rule #7

Let's Get Physical

"Too often we underestimate the power of a touch, a smile, a kind word, a listening ear, an honest compliment, or the smallest act of caring—all of which have the potential to turn a life around."

—Leo Buscaglia

When it comes to communication, studies show the major portion of our communication is through body language. It's the same with dogs—Harrison Forbes says in his book, *Dog Talk*, the leash is just an extension cord to our energy and emotions.

I think he's right. Much like kids, dogs look to us for our reaction to any situation as their cue about how to behave, or process the experience. They respond to body language first, tone of voice second, and actual words, third (yes, dogs have a vocabulary!) Good training and communication happens when all three signals—voice, body, and words—align perfectly, at the same time. When they do, dogs and people know EXACTLY what's expected, and they can perform perfectly. All you have to say is, "Do you want a cookie," or, "Do you want to go to the park," with a smile on your face and a song in your voice to get an idea of what happens when your dog reads all three of those signals correctly! It's really pretty cool . . .

As you're reading this, don't forget getting physical is more than touch—it's acknowledgment, recognition, and communication. We walk our dogs every day no matter what the weather—that's our promise to them and, every day, they remind us at the same time.

Maybe you know the saying, *if your dog is fat, you're not getting enough exercise.* It's true! When we lived in Vancouver, we committed to the dogs they would go to the forest twice a day. Now, with Barclay and Cheddar, we commit to playing in the morning, around noon, and at the end of work. Then, our big, family walk at eight o'clock in the evening. If we forget, they let us know! It makes me think about when I was raising my boys—I hope I was as thoughtful and receptive to their signals. I hope—when they asked to play—my answer was yes.

****

K2 were about as different from each other as two shepherds could get. Lana and I think Kaizer was more like me, whereas Katie was more like her. He was a tall, lopping, smell-the-roses kind of dog, whereas Katie was compact, precise, and task oriented. Their styles served well in search and rescue training because Kaizer was open field, and Katie was rubble pile.

What's the difference? Well, disaster or debris training involves working a pile of rubble when disaster hits, such as a tornado, hurricane, or earthquake. A dog and handler will work separately or together—depending on safety issues—to find survivors buried underneath rubble piles. Katie—who could dance on the head of a dime—was trained to use a bark alert, meaning she barked to indicate a live victim. She was trained to stay at her 'find' and bark, minimizing risk of injury to herself. She waited, and I went to her.

She was a more important asset than I.

Kaizer, on the other hand, was trained in open field as

a trailing dog. He did two things—trailing and tracking. Trailing dogs search for lost people, following a scent over long distances—a tracking dog is trained to follow a specific odor or scent. That's the primary skill set police forces need to track an individual. If K9 tracking dogs the police use find the person or felon, they're most likely trained to apprehend and bite. When Kaizer was working as a trailing dog, he was trained to lick the person's face with gusto to wake them up so he could get his reward or play toy. I called it, 'the Great Slobber Awakening!' Kids loved it, and many a boy scout had a clean face as a reward for being 'a find.'

Aside from work, Katie always had a sense of play. She bonked her ball into Kaizer's head or into his ball, as they got ready to go for a walk. She would come cruising through our legs from behind, then stop, so we had to pet her as we straddled her back. She'd bonk us with her ball, as well, as a way of saying "hurry up, let's go for a walk," or "I just want to hang out with you." Katie's sense of play was infectious and endearing. But, the truth?

Her sense of play paled compared to Dickens.

That puppy was a playing machine! He invented games, and then took on the task of teaching them to anyone willing to learn. The interesting thing for us was watching his unyielding patience. Often, the intent of his game was different from our expectation, and it took a lot of patience for us to get it right. Above all, he was a master at involving people in his day. Subtle, too. When a ball dropped on us from the second-floor landing, we were almost forced to engage!

Without nurturing, touch, and kindness, humans and animals will wither and die—physically and emotionally. At least, that's what studies show. Everyone knows when we're in love, the world looks different, we feel different, and people notice the difference in us. In other words, being in love or loving something, or someone, makes a huge difference in our lives. We're brimming with hope and optimism, as well as a host of other great emotions bringing us health and vitality.

When we love and are being loved, we look good every day.

****

When dogs—or, any animal—play, it's a form of getting physical. Whether bouncing a ball off of Skeeter's head, or running full on to give us a drive-by kiss, Dickens and all of our pets were physical.

So are we.

As time passed and our family changed, we still enjoy 'let's get physical' time with Barclay and Cheddar (as I read these words one more time, Cheddar is on a bar-high stool in our kitchen demanding to be scratched!) They make their wants known, and Lana and I find it impossible to walk by one of our pets without a quick touch, or hello.

It's a philosophy we live by with people and pets.

A touch on the arm, a brief smile—something. If you don't believe me, watch a litter of puppies wiggling all over each other, snoozing in a clump, and you'll know the importance of touch. Skeeter would reach out and touch us—or, a guest—with a gentle high five. Whenever we approached her, or if we were sitting on the couch and she wanted some attention, she would give us the high five.

Kaizer would stand still as I rubbed his forelegs up and down, and Katie loved to have her tummy rubbed while she was standing. Barclay gets a whole body rub in the morning before our day kicks in, and Cheddar? He jumps up on something to get as close as he can to look me in the eyes, asking for a bit of attention.

Here's what's really interesting—when it comes to interacting with each other, dogs ask for permission before the games begin. They first introduce themselves, obtain an okay to proceed, and respect the decision made—which may be a resounding NOT NOW! If we watch dogs that have a sense of play, they'll 'assume the position,' making invitation overtures. If the dog being asked to play reciprocates, the game is on. If it isn't, both dogs have established their boundaries, and the play doesn't happen.

Kind of sounds like us, doesn't it?

We tease, shove, and joke around as our invitation to play, but it's important to remember, sometimes, there's a resounding NOT NOW! When our dogs are working or are on leash, they don't always want to play. Why would they? They're busy! And, they make it known to whomever is asking, they're not interested at the moment.

Our sense of play is a great stress reliever, but we don't always follow our dogs' examples of asking for permission. There are environments where play and touch aren't welcomed, and everyone reacts differently. The trick is we need to understand the signals—our ability to read body language is one of the greatest skills we have for developing social interactions and emotional intelligence. Handshakes. Raised eyebrows. Body position. All telegraph what we're thinking and, when we understand the signals, we avoid possible conflict—it just makes sense. If understanding is communication's end result, Lana and I believe it's a good idea to study and learn what dogs take for granted—they ask for permission.

****

When dogs gather in groups, they establish order quickly among their ranks—not so with people. We often tend to cloud natural order with our own thoughts, feelings, and emotions. Dogs, however, deal with things in the moment, without worrying about what may be—for that reason, they discover order rapidly so they can get on with playing, or just being together.

The more I watch dogs, the more I understand some dogs are more social than others, and they desire more human or dog contact. Certain breeds of dogs love meeting everyone. Others? Being loved by a select few is okay with them! Dickens and Kaizer were like that, and Katie was the social butterfly. When Kaizer or Dickens hesitated, Katie moved forward to say hello, allowing children or adults to interact with her. But, she was selective—she didn't have the same desire to meet other dogs, nor was she interested in playing with them. As the saying goes, 'different strokes . . .'

Dickens? Easily bribed. Anyone with a ball who wanted to play, he was down with it! But, his 'other self' was a bit more reserved—kisses were reserved for family and best friends—nobody else had the pleasure. Barclay is the same way. Maybe it's because they received so much love and recognition from Lana and me when they were young and growing. They consistently received, loving looks, smiles, hellos, and touches throughout their lives, and interaction from others didn't matter.

As long as we loved them, they were just fine.

We're not so different. A gentle hand, a loving touch, or a kind word go a long way when it comes to connecting with someone. Lana has fond memories of times with Dickens when he sat beside her, seat belt fastened, going for a ride. She loved their one-on-one journeys, as well as the look of curiosity and contentment when he looked at her from his seat as if to say, "So, where are we going, Mom?"

Sometimes, he'd watch her as if memorizing every feature—she'd smile, say something gentle, and probably touch him. Maybe that was his intent all along. Who knows? I know it sounds like an inconsequential moment between owner and pet, but, really? It's so much more. Are we as physical with each other and our children as we are with our animals? I bet not—but, it should go without saying a well-intended touch is a welcomed touch. After all, who doesn't need a hug every now and then? Keep in mind, however, in a dog's world, unwelcome touch can result in a nasty bite, so it's prudent to pay attention to the dog's initial behavior. Welcoming, or unwelcoming?

Of course, if I don't bring cats into this equation, I'm pretty sure Cheddar will know it. It's a cat thing. So, before I get in trouble, I want to make it perfectly clear cats are people, too! Skeeter and Cheddar are great examples of cats who think they're a dog—Skeeter raised Dickens and, between the two of them, they shared cat and dog tendencies.

Aside from the obvious hug, kiss, handshake, bump, or pat on the head, we can touch lives in inconspicuous ways. I've seen people arrive at work, heading to their offices without saying hello to anyone—or, they walk down the halls, passing someone without acknowledging them. Or, they walk into a room, not looking at anyone. Remember, the things we don't do are also forms of communication and intent—they're just not positive. Think how different that scenario can be if only we take the time and initiative to acknowledge them . . .

The truth is we're more likely to touch an animal than another person. That said, we're probably more likely to say hello to homeless people sitting with a dog, than those who stand alone as we pass by. In our society, touch is almost a bad word because many people relate it to inappropriate behavior versus healthy interaction. Certainly, there's a time and place for everything, and touch must be welcomed. We would never walk up to a big dog and presume we have the right to touch it, nor should we do that to small dogs. Or, people.

We must wait for the signal.

Physical and emotional touch is imperative to our survival, but it must be permission based. Even if the dog is small, don't presume you can touch it—chances are you won't touch a ninety-pound dog you don't know, and the same goes for any dog of any size.

Ask first, and he or she may let you.

Size is an interesting perspective when it comes to touch. Hugging people or children who don't want to be held, touching employees, or taking advantage of physical size with anyone smaller are all issues of touch. Lana met a woman on one of her trips who always asked her small child permission for a hug. Sometimes her child said no—he was busy, and didn't want to be hugged. Not only that, he didn't want to be told he had to hug someone else. However, the woman also taught her son if he asked her for a hug, the answer was always going to be YES, and that was a very good feeling for both of them. Yes, she could have just locked him into a hug without asking, but you know what would have happened—the child would struggle to wriggle free, or not return the gesture in any way.

Now, I'm not suggesting we need to ask our children for permission to hug them—however, I'm pointing out we may impose our affections on others because we can, and at time when they don't really want it. We tend to approach large dogs with more respect than small dogs—do we do the same with people?

Permission-based touch is imperative and, most times, we automatically have our pet's permission. Who among us can walk by our pets without patting their heads, touching their ears, or scratching behind their collars? And, what a look we get when we do! My brother straddles his dog Suzie from the front facing backwards and stretches out her back legs, massaging them like two big 'ol ham hocks. Ha! She loves it, and gets a look of pure bliss on her face that says, "Don't stop!"

Welcome or invited touch is essential to communication. Shortly after we were married, Lana mentioned it seemed as if people stopped holding hands, or touching each other in public after they'd been married for a while. So, she requested I always continue to hold her hand even when we're old and gray, and always look at her when we toast a glass of wine. The best one, though? "Kiss me like you mean it!" All are issues of touch we want to have in our marriage, and I can hardly pass by Lana without a gentle touch for her. What can I say? It works for us—and, I bet it will work well for you, if you're willing to give it a shot.

By the way—if you see us walking down the street and we're not already holding hands, you have my permission to approach us, and place our hands together!

Rule #8

Live Your Passion

"Passion is energy. Feel the power that comes from focusing on what excites you!"
—Oprah Winfrey

66 Most men live lives of quiet desperation, and go to the grave with the song still in them." That's according to Thoreau.

I have to admit, that's a pretty strong observation. And, to be honest, I think of that quote when I work with people who feel they're in a dead-end job. Yes, I understand the feeling they may have to stay in their positions because of golden handcuffs—security, benefits, money. But, this is what I tell them . . . "Nobody holds a gun to your head, making you come to work."

We have choices, and the choice may be to wear those golden handcuffs. However, when it comes down to it, doing what you really want to do and having a vocation where you can truly do it is your choice. You can choose to follow your passion—or, not.

Dickens's passion was contagious—when he was playing, eating, or sleeping, he certainly did so with a zest for life! We could hear him drinking water from two rooms away, and he dove into his chow with unsurpassed gusto—we almost had to cover our ears! One time—you'll probably think we're weird—we made a recording of him, eating and, when we play it every now and then, we still laugh at his exuberance!

And, boy, could that dog bark! I used to bristle at it, but, once we recognized it was communicating his passion for something, we modified how we played with him. We agreed to a certain time frame when he had our undivided attention—he could live his passion without asking us to continue every time he dropped his ball.

That's how he lived his life—every day with purpose and passion. When he was in an agility class with Lana, he was so impatient, she decided to drop out because he couldn't sit still, waiting for his turn to express himself. That meant he wasn't having fun.

Watching K2 work was a wonder to behold and, on more than one occasion, if a family were watching us work, I sometimes approached them and asked if I could borrow their children. Seeing the surprised look on the parent's faces, I laughingly explained their kids were going to help me train my dogs for Search and Rescue. I'm sure the conversation on the way home for that family was full of pleadings to get a dog so they could do the same thing, as well as a little bit of wonder at the life of a working dog.

Maybe that's one reason I love dogs so much—they can't help but live their passion. Whether that passion is watching us so they don't miss an opportunity to do something, play their favorite game, or interact with us, they give us everything they have. Thoreau also said, "It's not what you look at that matters, it's what you see." Man—how true is that?

So, what do dogs see? Us. Their eyes follow us around the room, or stare at us, wondering and waiting—or, they cock their heads as they listen to our ramblings.

They. SEE. US.

When it comes to people, that doesn't mean when you're

living your passion, you can be so focused you miss what's happening around you. Knowing your passion simply gives you an opportunity to be aware of circumstances contributing to your passion—and, what opportunities are available, so you can share it with others. Together, I believe Lana and I are a successful couple because, with my awareness and her focus, there isn't much we miss, or anything we can't get done.

Another interesting observation? Our pets don't miss much—yet, sometimes, we miss everything. We go to work, and that's how we spend our days—or, nights. Then, we get home, sometimes not recalling what we did while we were at work. ARGHHH! To prove my point, see if you can remember what your colleagues were wearing yesterday at work. Most of us? We can't remember. For the most part, we relegate most of our day to situational numbness.

A sad state, to be sure.

How did we get ourselves into such a situation? Well— unlike dogs who smell the air, watch posturing, and listen to the sounds—we often plow through our days with blinders on. We aren't particularly good at looking around to see the learning opportunities right in front of our faces! In the book, *The Law of Attraction*, author Esther Hicks says,

"When you're tapped in, tuned in, and turned on, your power of influence and success is incredible." I believe that! Do you? When you know what you're supposed to be doing, there's no stopping you from achieving whatever you want. Knowing what you're good at—and, doing it—feels as effortless as walking.

That doesn't apply to only you—when we know what we want to do, we can see it and, by going after it, we live our passion. It's pretty simple, really—when we know the purpose and how our passion supports that purpose, everything becomes an opportunity to live our passion.

Dogs trained into a purpose already have the drive in their genes—it's up to a trainer to allow them to step into that gene-given role. Just watch German shepherds complete Schutzhund exercises, or a border collie herd sheep—or, a Boston terrier invent games. When there's purpose, there's passion—and, where there's passion, there's a ton of energy moving in the right direction. Others can't help getting swept up in the excitement as you live your way to success!

When we live our passion, it's tough to be someone we're not, and that fact shines through when we're choosing a dog. I believe we pick our dogs based on our passions, as well as on who we really are.

And, that's how Lana and I fell in love with Boston terriers—although, she did before me. I was a latecomer to the Boston terrier game.

"I fell into the Boston breed by accident," Lana explained one day, "when I was about eight years old. Later in life, I adopted the belief there are no accidents, so, I guess, Bostons and I were destined to meet—my family recently lost our cocker spaniel after spending a happy, fourteen-year life.

We were lost without a dog and, as a family, incomplete. Shortly thereafter, Dad heard of a family with dogs for sale— so, with sadness in our hearts and hope in our future, we headed off to meet our new dog.

The 'puppies' were older than we expected—almost five months—which was a concern. That wasn't a puppy! But, my dad was adamant about checking them out.

So, that's what we did.

If you're not familiar with a Boston terrier, let me fill you in—they're not furry bundles. They're bald, big-eyed, tailless, and nothing like any dog we'd ever seen. That bundle of baldness wasn't a dog, and we didn't want it!

Well, my dad wasn't having any of that! I'll be forever

grateful to him for his open-mindedness and insistence on bringing her home for the weekend. That was the deal— just have her for the weekend and, if we didn't want to keep her, he would take her back.

Perfect. We would send her home on Monday, then find a fluffy pup.

The short story? We named her Puggy, and she lived with us—or, we lived with her—for almost seventeen years! She was the best dog ever! She wanted to play all the time, she loved us and, since I was a little kid, when I chose to dress her in my doll clothes, her tail didn't get in the way of her wearing pants. What more could I ask?"

A quick aside—I wish you could see the look on Lana's face as she recounts her story to me . . .

"Years later," she recalled, "when it came time to add a dog to my cat filled, adult life, I looked for and found Dickens. He was two months old, and reminded me of a Mexican Toro Toro bull—filled with confidence, independent, and absolutely perfect for me.

He was me and I was him . . ."

You know, of course, we lost Dickens to cancer in 2005

and, to this day, we can be moved to tears with memories of his love, passion, and purpose. I often recognize his Boston tendencies in Lana's behaviors, and I smile at the thought of him. Memories will always be at our fingertips whenever Lana and I need them, and they still serve to fill us with inspiration, and love.

That's one heck of a legacy . . .

****

If you're disciplined and focused, you can quickly overcome someone who isn't. Sometimes, I find myself chasing after nothing which results from a lack of focus, goals, or discipline. When I recognize I'm doing it, I can hear Lana saying, "Focus, Honey," whenever I begin to stray from the task at hand. Sometimes, I wonder if I explored dog training because of the required focus to watch their behavior, and learn their motives. When a dog is on task or having fun with a purpose, their attention and energy are a wonder to behold! Maybe their focus helped me focus— sounds reasonable, don't you think?

When I work a dog, the whole world seems to disappear, and it's only me and the mouth-panting, ground-sniffing, eyes-imploring, tail-wagging, bundle of energy in front of me. When I work with dog owners, I teach them to train their dogs without thinking of what they look like to other people. The dog progresses rapidly because they—the owners—are listening to their dog that's in the moment with only one purpose.

Amidst that focus and discipline comes the most important lesson of all—if the reason for the intense concentration, focus, and drive isn't fun, you'll surely lose their attention. You know the saying, *if you do what you love, the money will follow."* With that in mind, find out what you're passionate about, and do it! Everything else will fall into place.

To this day, and after all of my years in organizational training, I still incorporate as much fun into my programs as I can. When we're having fun, time flies, and we're relaxed enough to absorb everything we hear, or do. Once in a while, I recall my past management career, and the one person whom I consider my mentor—a diminutive Italian guy named Jerry (now that I think about it, he really reminds me of Dickens—intense, disciplined, focused, and ready for a game any time, anywhere!) With a willingness to help me achieve and be my best, he helped me keep my interest and energy focused in the right direction.

But, what if a dog were my mentor? I'd learn things such as:

• When loved ones come home, always run to greet them.

• Never pass up the opportunity to go for a joyride.

• Allow the experience of fresh air and the wind in your face to be pure ecstasy.

• Take naps.

• Stretch before rising.

• Run, romp, and play daily.

• Thrive on attention, and let people touch you.

- Avoid biting when a simple growl will do.

- On warm days, stop to lie on your back on the grass.

- On hot days, drink lots of water, and lie under a shady tree.

- When you're happy, dance around, and wag your entire body.

- Delight in the simple joy of a long walk.

- Be loyal.

- Never pretend to be something you're not.

- If what you want lies buried, dig until you find it.

- When someone is having a bad day, be silent, sit close, and nuzzle them gently.

- ENJOY EVERY MOMENT OF EVERY DAY

- And, finally—live simply. Love generously. Care deeply. Speak kindly.

Sounds pretty good to me . . .

Rule #9

Manners Matter

"Respect for ourselves guides our morals—respect for others guides our manners."
—Laurence Sterne

How often have we commented on or heard someone else compliment a well-trained dog or a well-behaved child? There isn't a dog owner or parent who, upon hearing that, doesn't feel a sense of satisfaction and pride.

I will leave it to you to decide if good manners are common or not, but it seems to us the importance of teaching manners or practicing good manners takes a back seat in our busy lives. I'm not sure if we don't know what they look like, or if they simply aren't as important as they were to our parents and grandparents.

Regardless of the reason, it seems good manners aren't

universal or readily recognized. Many of us impose manners on our dogs that we don't impose on ourselves, or expect from others. The truth is, however, some dogs display behaviors we would do well to copy.

With my traveling experience, I've had the pleasure of stepping outside my norm into other worlds with different customs and traditions, and I know it's a big world. By observing pets and people throughout my travels, I had the opportunity to make a few comparisons, and the most important thing I learned? Improving or establishing manners requires awareness. It's wise to watch others, noticing what we admire and, equally important, what we don't admire. By being aware of both, we have an opportunity to adjust our behavior or point of view because, too often, we look for a one hundred percent change in one thing rather than a one percent change in one hundred things trying to change our behavior.

Our pets? Well, they're a different story. They're experts at noticing the one percent change, observing everything as they live life. Imagine if we paid as much attention to our surroundings, or to the people in our lives as they do! Pets use all of their senses—as well as being attentive to the small things—and, they don't miss a thing!

Being observant, attentive, and willing to grow is a good beginning to developing good manners, and I believe it's what we ask our pets to do as we walk them through their puppy kindergarten, and advanced obedience lessons (okay—total confession. I'm afraid I missed MY advanced obedience class, and now I'm learning as an adult!) As Lana and I worked through this rule, we found ourselves bristling at some of the observations—not because we disagreed with them, but because they stung.

They spoke the truth.

The more vehemently we reacted to a statement or personal observation of ourselves, the truer it tended to be— if the rule didn't speak the truth, it would roll off our backs like water. Now, we try to keep that in mind as we make our one percent changes throughout our lives—but, they rarely come without a little sting of truth and acceptance first.

Manners matter, and people usually notice them—in fact, they appear to stand out from the norm making them quite noticeable. Maybe you've already experienced it—as we increase our already frenzied lifestyles, we're moving away from traditional manners. For some reason, we're disinterested in taking the time to teach, and we achieve learning only by conscious effort. Many times, I spent time with dog owners, helping them train their pets to have exceptional manners, when, in fact, theirs were atrocious.

Part of my awareness came from moving to Canada—a place known for their politeness and manners. A place ridiculed by nations for being so polite. Don't you think that's a bit ironic? Is there such a thing as being too polite?

For many Americans, when they think of Canada and the USA, they assume all that divides them is a border—often referred to as the forty-ninth parallel. Other than that, they think we're basically the same. Not true! I discovered a different scenario when I moved to Vancouver from the United States. As an American—now, Canadian—I fondly refer to myself as an AmeriCanadian.

Now, it may mostly be Lana, but I found Canadians to be a society holding firmly onto British and European formalities, traditions, and manners. Lana is someone who notices manners in adults, children, and pets and they matter to her—therefore, they matter to me. I love learning, and I'm eager to make one percent changes toward my version of being a better person. Lana has a strong, manners-based foundation from her 'cowboy' upbringing—as well as her world traveling—but, she, too, is always willing to learn something new as she meets new people.

****

It started with Dickens.

I noticed it right away, when we went for a walk—he sat obediently, waiting for one of us to put on his leash. He healed on the left. He sat perfectly when we stopped at a street light. He never begged at the table when we were eating (until I started slipping him food—but, that's another story). He waited patiently for a treat, and took it gently. Dickens had manners and, because they mattered to Lana, she noticed and admired them in others. With my permission and a desire to grow, she began to share them with me.

I used to make Katie and Kaizer wait before they could dig into their food. However, it wasn't my habit to wait for everyone to receive their food before eating, nor was I trained to allow all the women at the table to order first. (As I said, we're going to have fun in this chapter! I'm not telling you our way is right—I'm simply sharing people notice manners-based behaviors!)

Since I chose to change my habits slightly, I always ask

women to order their beverage or meal first. I wait until everyone is served before eating. I stand if Lana or a woman sitting near me is arriving at, or leaving our table. Man! Those were some major changes! But, they were worth it—it's nice hearing appreciative comments from men and women! Not only that, good manners are contagious—and, that's a good thing (I know—I just sounded like Martha Stewart . . .)

As with people, you probably notice excellent manners in pets—a dog that comes when its called, heals beside you when it walks, stays when it's asked, and doesn't jump on guests is a pleasure to be around.

Out-of-control dogs are unbearable.

One more thing—manners apply to our children, as well. If you're anything like us, you know what it's like to visit friends or family, and you can't wait to leave because their children were unruly. Interrupting. Disrespectful. Clearly, the parents of those children aren't taking the time to train their children—and, they don't acknowledge or praise when their children do something right.

Every time our dogs do it right, we say, "Good sit!' Or, "Good come! Good stay!" It's the necessary positive reinforcement that works not only on dogs, but people, too. How about a heartfelt, "Thanks for being on time," or, "Thanks for coming home when you said you would!"

I know it sounds like a simple, little thing that could hardly make a difference. But, I promise you—practicing ongoing good manners—as well as acknowledging them—ensures they'll keep happening!

****

Too often, we notice or talk about what isn't working, not happening, or irritating us rather than looking for the positive or good in a situation. In short, we're problem solvers rather than solution finders—which means we're focusing on the problem.

When teaching manners, focusing on the positive is

imperative. Complimenting and recognizing what's done well is critical. Next time you compliment your dog for a good sit, look at its face. Our dog wiggles all over, and I'm sure he smiles!

If you're young—and, I mean younger than Lana or I—I recognize we're from a different generation, but we stand by our belief some good, old-fashioned manners would do this world well. For instance, the proper use of cutlery—how to hold a fork and cut with a knife without looking like the meat is going to escape if it's not stabbed with a vengeance. It's one of the areas where a one percent change can make a huge difference.

Again, I take it back to our dogs. Cats. Critters. Take notice—how do they interact with you? For many of us, a huge change is what people notice. We can walk down the hallway at work and say hello to someone, asking them how they are, and we'll get the usual response. "Good." Or, "Okay. "Unless they have a patch on one eye, or are sporting crutches, it's unlikely we'll notice any differences. So, why is it we're always looking for BIG CHANGES?

Doesn't it make more sense to start small? Try taking on a one percent change, and look for the same in others. Try to remember what your coworkers were wearing yesterday.

Most of us can't unless, for some reason, we gave it some attention or significance. Give it a shot—it's an interesting challenge to improve your observation skills—try making positive observations when the opportunity presents itself.

Another behavior we practice is giving our attention in the moment. Have you ever paid attention to what happens when you walk into a room in which your dog already claimed space? Have you noticed what they do whenever you speak to them? Try it. I guarantee, they'll look at you. Now, try it with your spouse, your kids, or a work colleague.

Not so much.

I think it ultimately boils down to respect. If you speak to a person, look at him or her. If people speak to you, show them respect by paying attention to what he or she has to say. Look them in the eye. Trust me—dogs do it all the time, and we take it for granted. When we smile at them, their ears assume the position of a smile in return—for Dickens and Kaizer, the ears went back. Katie? They stayed up. The same with Barclay—when we talk to him, he's always trying to figure out what we're saying. Or, he's listening for a command or words he recognizes, such as 'cookie,' or 'park.'

I won't mention . . . 'squirrel.'

Skeeter was the same. She liked to perch on the pillows on our bed and, if she heard us enter the room, she'd raise her head, let out a little chirp hello, and look directly at us to acknowledge our presence. To be acknowledged instantly was a nice feeling! That's the way it is with most pets—they don't wait until they finish typing or texting someone. They acknowledge us the moment we arrive . . .

Similar to a healthy human relationship that others want to be around, teaching our dogs manners is imperative to a harmonious household—as I mentioned, many of us dedicate more time to teaching them manners than focusing on our own. Etiquette is the rule of behavior in certain situations, whereas having good manners is showing kindness and consideration to others. It's about making people feel good about themselves, and it makes us feel good, too. If we can teach our dogs to wait for us to go in the gate first, go up the stairs after we do, or wait until we open the door, we can certainly show others the same respect and consideration.

Rule #10

Take Time for Rest and Play

I work hard, and I tend to play hard. I very seldom rest hard.

—*Jacqueline Bisset*

Have you noticed a constant point of discussion in our culture is about the need to be less busy, less planned, and make time for exercise and rest?

Maybe we should look to cats for the answer.

You gotta admit there's no better example of the art of rest than a cat—I think it's inherent in all of them. Skeeter was certainly a champion of and queen of the cat nap, and Cheddar would make her proud.

Barclay, too. An afternoon snooze is a good way to pass a little time!

So, while sit comes naturally to Cheddar and Barclay, we approach rest as a structured activity, resisting it for its non-productivity. Nothing could be further from the truth! There's a business concept known as a beta/alpha state, which means 'productive nothingness.' Software giants pioneered the concept for their employees, so they would TAKE TIME TO REST in order to be as productive as possible.

I like to read at night before I go to sleep, and, when I'm reading, my brain is in a beta state. When I put my Nook down, turn off the lights, and close my eyes, my brain moves from beta to alpha, then to theta. Finally, when I fall asleep, I reach delta—a deep, dreamless sleep (we dream in a theta state.) Barclay can be chasing his ball and, when we're done with the game, he lies down and is dreaming in a theta state or snoring in a delta state within minutes. Wouldn't that be nice if we could do the same thing? Oh, if only we could be dogs!

Cheddar? Delta state all day long, dead to the world!

Our dogs have taught us to take advantage of a nap. Whether on the trail, in the car, or in the back yard, all of them would grab a nap whenever they could, while we kept to our frantic pace.

Rest is a core component of a balanced life and fitness routine. Giving your body time to recover between exercises, after a workout or through extended periods, will help it replenish energy and recover from strain. According to Harvard Medical School, additional benefits of rest include increased concentration, memory function, and overall mood.

When it comes to rest, animals seem to know something we don't, and I want to know what that is! I touch it briefly when I take a moment to sit with them and watch the world go by—rest doesn't mean sleep. It means slowing down, maybe putting down our electronics, disengaging from the world for a while. Most of us are overworked, over stressed, over busy and, sometimes, we're doing that to our children. Are we keeping them as busy as we are, or giving them space to do nothing? Are we teaching them it's okay to slow down like our pets do?

When we're playing with Barclay, it seems like he'll play forever and, the more we play, the more tired he gets. Without rest, he seems to get overtired, and begins to bite on (rather than play with) his toys, our hands and, on occasion, his brother. When that happens, we call it quits, and everyone powers down.

Shouldn't we do the same thing?

Yes, but that takes discipline, and we're working on it—with his help.

I'm beginning to listen.

All of our dogs have consistently demanded exercise or play time. They want to play, go to the forest for a walk, chase a ball, or go for a run. Cheddar, too, wants out the door for a walk when the cool of the evening hits. They're smart about it, though—they don't want to go during the heat of the day. In the morning, when it's cool, or at the end of the day they get restless, and it's time to move.

If we look at the wisdom of our pets, or of animals in general, unlike humans, they never voluntarily exercise or play during the heat of the day. Watching people cycling, or running with a panting dog at their side when the sun is high is a painful sight. Of course, the dogs don't want to disappoint us, so they go along, doing their best to keep up. Still, without exception, they know we should be waiting until it's cooler.

Never minding the weather, Barclay and Cheddar need to play. The wiggles must happen, and they're good for them! I confess, however, on many occasions we prefer to stay seated in front of a good movie. Nonetheless, aware of the yearning look on their faces, we start to move, and we're a better family for it. Remember—if your dog is fat, you're not getting enough exercise!

If you have trouble hauling yourself off the couch, pick a time when you are the most mentally relaxed. Lace up the running shoes. Pick a walking route. Anything. Then, do it for one month—every day. If it doesn't help you physically, mentally, and spiritually, sit down with your dog, and tell him you need help.

I'm sure you'll get it!

Rule #11

Have Great Expectations

"A wonderful gift may not be wrapped as you expect."

—Jonathan Lockwood Huie

In July of this year, Lana and I traveled to my family reunion in Colorado for about a week. We expected to leave the pets at home with our live-in dog sitter since they couldn't come with us.

Barclay and Cheddar didn't know what to expect.

Or, did they?

Expectations can be viewed in a couple of ways—first, our pets have to wait for us to return. Better yet, I believe they expect us to return. But, unlike us, they don't have any idea of when we'll be home—they just expect us to be home.

Sometime. That's why they get so darned excited when we walk in the door—expectation met! Since they live in the moment and not in the future, they're never disappointed because their expectations are usually met.

Second, the word 'expectation' brings with it an aspirational focus that keeps driving us forward. If we expect great things to happen, they usually do. If we expect bad things to happen, they usually do. How many times have you said, "It's going to be one of those days"—and, it is! Why? Because you said it would be, and you expected it to be one of those days. However, our animals can't do that—their day is always the best day they can make it. They all ways have great expectations.

Wouldn't that be nice?

Remember what I told you about Cheddar? He showed up one day at the trucking company of our brother-in-law. He (Cheddar, not our brother-in-law) was skinny, hungry, with an eye infection and covered in grease. He was skittish, mistrustful, and starving—a combination of tendencies making it easy for us to decide what he was NOT going to be as he moved forward in his life. Instead, we decided he made his way to us for a reason—to be a great cat living a remarkable life.

Living in a home with a large back yard enclosed by a tall wooden fence, we knew if Cheddar were allowed to go outdoors, he'd be gone. We wanted different things—his desire was to explore, and we wanted him safe. So, we came up with a compromise—a cat fence, a leash, and a bell.

For our first attempt at a cat fence, we created a type of 'top of the fence' enclosure that ran along the fence top to help keep him in the backyard. Next, we clipped a thirty foot tracking lead to his collar, and attached a bell so we could hear him if we couldn't see him. So began his life on a leash.

He learned to love that thirty-foot lead.

The combination of the fence, leash, and bell became his expectation he was free to roam. Today, in our new home, we have a much more sophisticated cat fence, as well as a doggy-kitty door that lets him come and go into the back yard. Cheddar expects the leash means going for a walk, and now asks (demands) his leash be put on because he knows he'll go for a walk! Yes!

He's a clever kitty, walking on leash with or without Barclay. We raise eyebrows daily, sometimes getting our picture taken as we walk our neighborhood. He loves adventures, and they come on the end of a leash. You know how cats aren't supposed to walk on a leash? Well, they do if you have great expectations for them!

That brings me to the question—do we expect different results from people based on their neighborhood? What if they're physically or mentally challenged? What if they're poor? Do we decide their potential based on the right or wrong side of the tracks? When we expect the worst, do we look for them to prove us right? Do we limit our expectations for others based on our own successes or failures? Or, do we see the sky as the limit, and encourage them to greatness? I believe dogs expect the best of everyone and deal with whatever they get.

Barclay and Cheddar, like us, are willing to try just about anything. Their latest adventure is going for a ride in the buggy behind my bike. Lana, the ever-cautious mom, wasn't sure if Cheddar would want to go for a ride, but, in the end, he enjoys it more than Barclay, stretching out, watching the world fly by.

Then—cars. Cheddar loves feeling the wind in his fur, the spring air . . . okay, that's a little much. But, from day one, he seemed comfortable in our car. Maybe he knew he was coming home, but, like Skeeter before him, our expectation was he was going to be a traveling man. We started with short drives, ending with a cat treat which, for him, was a positive experience. Now, he rides in his crate that's bungeed to the seat, so he, Lana, and I are safe.

And, a travelin' man he is! Cheddar has traveled across Western Canada and as far south as Oregon, his adventures taking him to posh places such as the Fairmont Banff Springs Hotel. Oh, yeah—he had his own bed. And, dishes.

Traveling seems to be in his blood, and he loves his adventures! I can't tell you how many times people tell us their cat doesn't like to ride in the car. My response? "Where have you taken them besides the vet?" Their response? "Nowhere."

Well, if the only car ride I took was to the dentist, I wouldn't like car rides either. Again, it comes down to expectations—they have them for you, don't they?

Do you have great expectations for them?

****

Based on the greeting we get when we walk through the door, we imagine our pets also have great expectations of us—perhaps something as simple as their expectation of our arriving home. Or, to play. Or, in Cheddar's case, to be fed. We can only imagine, based on their greeting when we walk through the door, they KNEW we would come back to them.

A further, interesting note about Cheddar—in our desire to nourish him from his skinny, four-pound self to a healthy twelve-pound feline, I think we created a chow hound. His great expectation is that he won't be hungry again. He celebrates our return home with a run to his food dish—which is on top of the dryer—and, with him at chest level, he loves us in his special way. Just the way he loves his food. It's a close, bonding experience to meet his great expectation of his never being hungry again. He loves to eat and, to keep him at a healthy weight, we measure out his daily food rationing in a measuring cup. If we let him eat when he wanted, he would become a garbage disposal, and begin to look like Garfield!

Barclay, on the other hand, must be convinced to eat, as did Dickens. Neither were food driven—they only had toys on their minds! Barclay has serious expectations for his play schedule, and we find it impossible to disappoint!

It's weird how every animal is different, isn't it?

Dogs expect things to work out, and become balanced and peaceful. You might know already that if you ever walked a dog on a leash and experienced an unpredictable situation—your expectations of the outcome transmits down the lead. Your dog behaves differently on leash than it does off leash. Why? Because your expectations (transmitted by leash) are different than their expectations given that situation. Left alone (no leash), your dog has expectations that the situation will evolve into a harmonious situation given the unspoken, yet undeniable, pack order.

With dogs, that's the way it is.

It will never change.

Final Thoughts

If you want to experience the best of life, people, and your pets, try building your relationships like a dog!

—Richard Casavant

So, there you have it! Lana and I hope our little book helps you understand dog behavior, and how it relates to your everyday life. There's really no secret to creating a healthy, happy life for you, your friends, and family. Well, maybe there is—one which you now know . . .

Build relationships like a dog.

It works!

PROFESSIONAL ACKNOWLEDGMENTS

CHRYSALIS PUBLISHING AUTHOR SERVICES
L.A. O'Neil, Editor
chrysalispub@gmail.com
www.chrysalis-pub.com

HIGH MOUNTAIN DESIGN
Wyatt Ilsley, Cover Design
hmdesign89@gmail.com
www.highmountaindesign.com

89130972R00080

Made in the USA
Columbia, SC
11 February 2018